1966 and All That

1966
and All That

★

CRAIG BROWN

ILLUSTRATIONS BY KEN PYNE

A History of Modern Britain comprising all the parts you can almost remember including an Unsuitable King, one too many Gathering Storms and a good half-dozen Unmemorable Prime Ministers.

HODDER

Hodder & Stoughton

Copyright © Craig Brown 2005
Illustrations © Ken Pyne 2005

First published in Great Britain in 2005 by Hodder and Stoughton
A division of Hodder Headline

The right of Craig Brown to be identified as the Author
of the Work has been asserted by him in accordance
with the Copyright, Designs and Patents Act 1988.

A Hodder & Stoughton Book

1 3 5 7 9 10 8 6 4 2

A CIP catalogue record for this title is
available from the British Library

ISBN 0 340 89711 2

Typeset by Palimpsest Book Production Limited,
Polmont, Stirlingshire
Printed and bound by Clays Ltd, St Ives plc

Hodder Headline's policy is to use papers that are natural,
renewable and recyclable products and made from wood grown in
sustainable forests. The logging and manufacturing processes are expected
to conform to the environmental regulations of the country of origin.

Hodder and Stoughton Ltd
A division of Hodder Headline
338 Euston Road
London NW1 3BH

For my children, Tallulah and Silas

'History is just one bloody thing after another'

Sir Herbert Butterfield (1900–1979),
Professor of Modern History at
Cambridge University.

'A great deal was happening everywhere, and people were certainly aware of it. It was regarded as a good thing when we were the ones doing it, and aroused apprehensiveness when it was done by others. Every schoolboy could understand each thing as it happened, but as to what it all meant in general, nobody really knew except for a very few persons, and even they were not sure. Only a short time later it might well have happened in a different sequence, or the other way round, and nobody would have known the difference, except for a few changes that inexplicably establish themselves in the course of time and so constitute the slimy track made by the snail of history'

Robert Musil,
The Man Without Qualities

CHAPTER 1

THE END

CHAPTER 2

The Beginning of the End

History ended on 31 December 1918. It was the end of an error.

CHAPTER 3

The End of the Beginning of the End

History began again on 1 January 1919. It was the dawn of a new error.

THE TWENTIES

An Irresponsible Decade

In the Twenties everybody lets down their hair, chances their arm and puts their best foot forward, only to find themselves in it up to their necks.

At Sandringham, King George V feverishly turns back the clocks; in Arabia, Lawrence tries to blend in by looking sheepish on a camel; and in Dublin, Yeats joins the 'Ni' Crowd.

It is the decade of colourful cocktails and risqué dances, of family-planning clinics and the Bloomsbury Grope; the decade in which Yogi Bear invents the BBC, Bonar becomes Law, and Labour Prime Minister Ronald MacDonald engages in a struggle on behalf of the upper class; an irresponsible decade that spends far too much time out on the razzle, and too little time realising that, in only a matter of years, the Twenties will give way to the Thirties.

CHAPTER 4

Everybody Has Fun

To get over the Great War, the people of Britain decided to enjoy themselves.

King George V had fun by sticking stamps in his album and marching round Sandringham in single file turning back the clocks.

The Palace historians warned him that no one can turn back the clocks. But the King proved them wrong. He kept the clocks at Sandringham exactly a century behind Greenwich Mean Time. This meant he was always early for appointments.

King George's wife, Queen Mary, enjoyed herself by visiting antique shops and hoovering up the window displays into her big pockets. She emerged from each shop to cheers from the crowds. Each time she waved back, great piles of glass and cutlery and precious stones would clatter to the pavement.

Honours for Sale

King George's oldest son, Lloyd, enjoyed himself selling honours out of a suitcase on the street, at a price to suit all pockets. Anyone who wasn't anyone was able to purchase honours for themselves and their children. Titles dating from this time, in order of precedence, include:

Duke Ellington
Duke of Earl
Dukes of Hazzard
The Duchess of Duke Street
Count Basie
Count Down
Brighton Peer
Lord Luvaduck
Lord E. Bee
Lady Luck
Lord and Lady Muck
Big Sir
Sir Cus
Sir Plus
Knight Train
Knight Porter
Hon. Oakley Moor P'Tat
Hon. de Wear

An Unmemorable King

King George V was dull but dependable. He never asked much of life. At the start of his reign, he grew a beard. He spent the rest of his reign keeping it in trim.

He was not full of imagination. While visiting severely wounded soldiers in hospital during the Great War he coined the two great questions that have been asked by the Royal Family of everyone ever since: 'Have you come far?' and 'What are you doing here?'

King George V will be remembered for failing to say or do anything at all memorable. The only thing anyone can remember about him is his last words. They were either: 'How is Bognor?' or 'Bugger the Empire!' But no one can remember.

CHAPTER 5

The Social Order Is Restored

The Twenties had hardly begun when the Labour Party came to power under Ronald MacDonald, the illegitimate son of a fast-food salesman.

Upon hearing the news, King George V was terrified that the new Prime Minister would stink out the Palace and spend his time in the Palace kitchens stirring up discontent.

The King was desperate to keep Ronald MacDonald on side, so he hired a labourer's uniform to welcome him to the Palace. Carrying a chimney brush and a whippet, clad in grubby overalls, a flat cap and clogs, his face blackened with soot, King George was taken aback to find Ronald MacDonald on bended knee, dressed up to the nines in top hat, white tie and tails.

The King breathed a sigh of relief. He suggested that he and MacDonald might feel more comfortable switching uniforms. Within seconds, revolution was averted and the social order was restored.

A Legendary Figure

D. H. Lawrence of Arabia was a legendary figure who rode around on a camel in the Arab section of Nottingham. But he liked to come home to a warm fire, and wrestle naked men.

He is best remembered today for his groundbreaking books *Seven Pillows for Women*, *Camels in Love* and *Lady Chatterbox's Llama*. The latter was banned for many decades owing to its many explicit passages describing Lady Chatterbox's attempts to mount her Llama:

> 'Tha's got such a nice tail on thee. Tha's got a real soft sloping bottom on thee. It's a bottom as could hold the world up, it is. An' if tha shits and if tha' pisses, I'm glad. I don't want a woman as couldna shit nor piss. Tha'rt real, tha art! Here tha shits and here tha pisses: an' I lay my hand on 'em both an' like thee for it.'

D. H. Lawrence of Arabia Forsakes Fame

Lawrence was famous for turning his back on fame. He strove for anonymity, and was often to be seen walking up and down Oxford Street wearing a board on which was written in bold capitals '**I AM NOT WHO YOU THINK I AM.**'

He was a master of disguise. Among his most popular alter egos were:

Ross, D.E.: lead singer with the Supremes, who finally split with fellow group members Ursula and Gudrun, citing 'musical differences'.

Shaw, Aircraftsman Sandy: chart-topping 1968 Eurovision Song Contest winner. Eagle-eyed observers were able to guess Shaw's true identity from the tell-tale way in which he bared his feet in public, Bedouin-style.

CHAPTER 6

The Jazz Age

In the mid-Twenties, Britain became entranced by All Things American. Overnight, everybody littered their conversation with the latest Americanisms, like 'makin' whoopee', 'hot diggity dawg' and 'big cheese'.

Nightclubs and drinking parlours opened on every street corner. Barmen mixed decadent new cocktails while dancing the Hokey Cokey.

Even the highest in society were not immune to this craze. This may be detected in this extract from King George V's Christmas broadcast, 1925:

Through one of the marvels of modern Science, I am enabled, this Christmas Day, to speak – hic! – to all my peoples throughout the Empire. Well, hot diggity dawg. It may be that our future will lay upon us more than one stern test. Ain't that just the bee's whiskers? For the present, the work to which all us diggity dawgs are equally bound is to arrive at a reasoned tranquillity within our borders – hic! – and so let's make hot cheese. I speak now from my home and from my heart to you all. Get hot! Daddi-o! Get hot! To all – to each – I wish a happy Christmas. Gee whiz! Thanks for the buggy ride, and God – hic! – bless you all.

The Dance Craze

Nightclubs and cocktail bars opened up across the country, and became home to all the latest dance crazes. The two most popular were:

The Rumba
1 measure of coconut milk to 2 measures of rum.
  Shake, rattle and roll.
  Then pour.

The Charleston
Swivel on the balls of the feet, balance pigeon-toed.
  Sway the body from side to side, knocking the knees with both hands.
  Collapse.

In the Embassy Club in London, the young Prince of Wails drank highballs and performed a wicked Charleston. There were similar hotspots all over Britain, every bit as glamorous. The 'in' crowd in Leeds would flock to the Cloggie Club to drink the fashionable new Buttie Cocktail and dance the Morris.

Le Cocktail Buttie
I chip buttie to 2pts Brown Ale.
   Mash and mix.
   Pour into dainty glass. Top off with cocktail umbrella and galoshes.

CHAPTER 7

The Birth of the BBC

The BBC was discovered by John Yogi Bear and his assistant Boo-Boo while they were experimenting in his attic with two cardboard boxes and a length of wire.

By moving one box slightly to the right, Yogi Bear found that a man in a dinner jacket and black tie could appear in the other box, reading the latest news headlines, and saying, *'This is the BBC from London.'*

The head of the BBC was a Scottish undertaker called John Wreath, later Lord Wreath.

Wreath insisted that everyone appearing on the wireless had to wear a dinner jacket and black tie. This explains why the British fared so poorly in the 1926 Olympics, particularly in the synchronised swimming, from which – tragically – five of the team never returned.

For the first thirty years of its life, the BBC refused to

broadcast. Lord Wreath insisted that the British people had much better things to do with their time than sit around eavesdropping on complete strangers.

But finally, Lord Wreath relented. He let the following three programmes be broadcast, but only on strict condition that listeners sat up straight and behaved themselves:

1. *The Royal Christmas Broadcast*

   In which King George V talks the nation through his stamp collection and tidies it away before wishing them a Satisfactory Christmas. Sadly the King's 1928 message to the nation was not broadcast. Queen Mary had pocketed it.

2. *A Round or Two of Pelmanism*

   Lord Wreath shuddered at the idea of quiz shows, but for five years he let '*A Round or Two of Pelmanism*' be broadcast for three hours a week, as the Saturday highlight. It consisted of four unknown players in full military attire participating in a few rounds of Pelmanism in silence, without commentary.

   It gripped a nation that had, up to that moment, been forced to make its own entertainment.

3. *The News*

   Under Lord Wreath, the BBC broadcast news only when there was news worth broadcasting. This meant there was no news from 1922 to 1925, or from 1927 to 1928, and only one brief news broadcast in 1929. It concerned the Wall Street Crash. 'It has been reported to us that there has been some sort of mild upset in New York,' said the announcer, 'but happily no Britons were involved.'

CHAPTER 8

The Arts in the 1920s

The Twenties was a time of great leaps forward in the world of literature. From America came *The Waste Land* by T. S. Eliot. From Ireland came *Ulysses* by James Joyce. From France came *À La Recherche du Temps Perdu* by Marcel Proust. And from England came *Now We Are Six* by A. A. Milne.

The British preferred to let the aristocracy preside over the avant-garde to ensure it remained in keeping and traditional.

The Spitwells

The Spitwell family were celebrated for being aristocratic and eccentric. Osbert, Nosbert, Rosbert, Cosbert, Snosbert and Flosbert devoted their mornings to being aristocratic and their afternoons to being eccentric.

Meanwhile their sister, Edith Spitwell, entranced London with her poem 'Facile' reciting it to music by the extinguished composer Ralph Vaughan Walt William Walton.

The Bloomsbury Grope

The Bloomsbury Grope was the name given to a tightly knit bunch of friends (latterly former friends) who moved into one another's bedrooms and bathrooms with a view to knitting tightly. Some were nits; others were tight; a few were both. They all kept dairies.

The Bloomsbury Grope consisted of Virginia Woof, Lord Carrington, Roger Fry-Up, Arse Longa Vita Sackville-West, Lytton Stretchy, Dr Forster of Gloucester, Vanessa Hell, Lady Utterly Quarrel and Milton Keynes, a new town divided against itself.

Of these, Carrington was the only one to resign after admitting having made a mistake.

The Grope's members were all in love with one another. But sadly no two were in love with each other at the same time.

They were left-wing in outlook, believing that the old order had had its day.

As the sensitive Woof wrote in her dairy: 'How I wish ours

was a world free of the servant class! It is so very *tiresome* to be waited upon by people so coarse and grubby and unread.'

W. P. B. Yeats

W. P. B. Yeats singlehandedly revived Celtic folklore by placing 'ni' everywhere.

His romantic ni heroine, Cathleen ni Houlihan, wandered through the Celtic ni Twilight re-creating Irish ni Legends.

Yeats was fond of the aristocratic country-house life, which was the in ni spiration for perhaps his fi-ni-st work, 'A ni One For Ten ni S?'.

Was the element of natio ni lism in his plays too strong? Some histor ni ans argue that his work ni progress nispired ruthless foreigners like Leni and, of course, Mussolini.

Throughout his life, Yeats was in love with Maud; but before he knew it, she was Gonne.

CHAPTER 9

Ronald MacDonald Settles In

By the end of his sixteen-course meal in Buckingham Palace with King George V and Queen Mary, Ronald MacDonald discovered he had changed his mind about the workers sharing the means of production.

From now on, he felt it better that the Dukes and

Duchesses should share the means of production. The workers would just have to make do with whatever was left.

CHAPTER 10

America Tries to Inch Ahead but Fails

In the 1920s, America tried to inch ahead of Britain, but Britain wasn't having it.

First, it was reported that Charles Iceberg and Amelia Earwig had flown single-handedly across the Atlantic. This upset the British, who had known how to fly single-handedly across the Atlantic for years, but hadn't got round to it. On further investigation, it was discovered that both the Americans had flown in aeroplanes, which didn't really count.

America in the 1920s gave birth to movie stars, baseball, skyscrapers, jazz and world domination. But Britain continued to be much better at Cricket. And, furthermore, Britain was much, much better at not boasting.

CHAPTER 11

Winston Changes Sides

Winston Churchill was young right up until he was old.

In the 1920s, he kept changing sides. This kept him young. 'I say this in the strongest possible terms as a Liberal,' he would thunder in the House of Commons. Then he would change sides. 'And I reply in the strongest possible terms as a Conservative.'

'As a Liberal, I demand to intervene!'

'Sir, this Conservative objects to your intervention!'

Fortunately, the only other MP in the House of Commons in those days was Ronald MacDonald, who was generally out taking tea with Duchesses.

The General Strike

The General Strike occurred when all the Generals went on Strike.

The Generals had been kept busy in the war to end all wars but when that war came to an end it looked as though there might be no more wars so they kicked up a fuss.

The British public rallied round, taking on General jobs they had never been trained for. These included:

General Maintenance
General Well-being
General Purpose
General Knowledge
General Idea
General Furore
General Nuisance
General Motors

Birth Control

In London, the first Family Planning Clinic was begun by Marie Stop.

For the first time in living memory, the British came face to face with sex. They did not like what they saw.

Sex had only occurred in the nation's history three times before. It had always ended in tears.

The Causes and Outcomes of Sex in Britain, 1066–1920

  (i) *King Henry VIII.* The overweight monarch had sex with Anne Boleyn. He then put the blame on her and ordered her to be beheaded.

 (ii) *Samuel Peeps.* The famous diarist admitted to having sex on several occasions, but never in clear prose.

(iii) *Joan of Ark.* Joan of Ark never had sex. Nor was she British. So she doesn't count.

Howard Crater discovered his mummy in the Tomb of Tooting Common in Eejit. The second his mummy opened up the coffee he was cursed.

Within fifty years, everyone on the expedition to uncover the Tomb of Tooting Common had either a) died *or* (b) grown old *or* (c) grown old and died.

The treasures uncovered by Crater were removed from Tooting Common and placed in the British Museum, where they were known as the Elgin Marbles.

There were calls to place them back in Tooting Common, but Elgin did not want to lose his marbles so they stayed put.

CHAPTER 12

Memorable Dates in the 1920s

There were no memorable dates in the 1920s.

The Twenties

Answer THREE questions, choosing ONE from Section A, ONE from Section B, ONE from Section C and ONE from Section D.

You are advised to spend half the time on Section A that you spend on Section B, three-quarters of the time on Section C that you spend on Section D, and twice the time on Section D that you spend on Section A.

Do not spend any time on Section E. There is no Section E.

1 (a) Do you agree or disagree with this statement?
  (b) How has your attitude to this question changed since you first read it?

Please turn over before answering the next question.

2 (a) Imagine you are a member of the Bloomsbury Grope. Give reasons.
  (b) When, what or who did Bonar Law? And why?

Answer the next question making full use of the pocket calculator you didn't bring with you because you thought you wouldn't need it.

3 (a) Subtract the 50 per cent duty imposed on German goods by the Reparation Recovery Act of 1921, the year in which it passed into law. Divide the figure by the number

of goals scored by Bolton Wanderers against West Ham in the 1923 FA Cup Final, and multiply in time for the All-India Congress.

You may spend no more than two seconds on the next question. Your time is up.

4 (a) The League of Nations came into existence in January 1920. What was its name?

   (b) Imagine you have just bought a peerage for yourself from Boy George for £80,000. This leaves you with just one shilling (1/-) to buy somewhere to live. That won't get you very far, will it? Well, it's too late to do anything about it now. Why didn't you think of it before you wasted all that money?

   (c) (Why is this question in brackets?)

5 Study Diagram C and then answer **all** parts of Question 5. But not this one, as it is not a question.

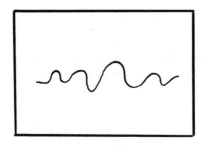

(a) Which of the following statements is applicable to Diagram C?

   (i) The upper edge of a stamp in the Royal Collection has even perforations.

   (ii) A choppy sea greets reinforcements in the occupation of Constantinople.

   (iii) Boy George's smile falters when he is faced with accusations of abusing the honours system.

NAZI SECTION (COMPULSORY)

   (i) Did the General Strike cause Hitler's inexorable rise to power?

   or

   (ii) Did Hitler's inexorable rise to power cause the General Strike?

NB Answer both questions at the same time, taking special care to come to different conclusions.

In what ways did *either* The Bloomsbury Grope *or* John Yogi Bear contribute to Hitler's inexorable rise to power? Compère and contrive.

THE THIRTIES

An Anxious Decade

Historians are generally agreed that the Thirties come shortly before the Forties, but immediately after the Twenties. This lends the Thirties a definite sense of being hemmed in on both sides.

It is a prurient decade, a decade in which some people pull back the blinds and peer out, only to see others peering in. As leading historian Eric Hobbskettle points out, it becomes, in a very real way, the Age of Uncurtained Teas.

CHAPTER 13

The Birth of Reggie

Russ Tafari, also known as Reggie, a musician, became Emperor Haile Salacious of Abyssinia. He composed the popular songs, 'So long, Abyssinia', 'Abyssinia On My Return' and 'Abyssinia After All These Years'.

After enduring years of attacks from puns on all sides, Emperor Haile Salacious fled his country, and lay low in a bath. He is now regarded as a saint for suffering outrageous puns so long. Ten thousand people attended his funeral, which was suitably solemn.

'You could have heard a pun drop,' remarked one observer.

A Poor Reception

Over in Germany, a young moustachioed painter was having trouble selling his landscapes. Kindly passers-by took him to one side and advised him they might sell better were he to remove the troops and military hardware from the fore-ground. But his only response was to start shouting at them.

Sir Oswald's Muesli

Back in Britain, Sir Oswald was repeatedly dissatisfied with his muesli. He could not swallow all the different bits and pieces.

So he left every party he joined. But that didn't work so he joined every party he left. Then he changed tactics and left every party *before* he joined it. Finally he created a new party just for himself. After heated discussion with himself, he decided to call it the New Party. After a show of hand, the title was accepted, with one abstention.

Sir Oswald went around the country stirring up discontent within himself. The New Party would be, he said, the Party of Action. But then he lowered his sights to something more realistic: from now on, it would be the Party of Acton.

Exasperated by his increasing exasperation, Sir Oswald then made a bold, decisive move. He left his old party, the New Party, and founded a new New Party, the British Union of Florists.

As Life President of the British Union of Florists, Sir Oswald travelled up and down the country giving demonstrations to halls packed full of his fellow Florists.

He became known for raising his hand to its fullest height then banging it down on whatever arrangement was in front of him. But this was not the British way so Sir Oswald was put behind bars.

CHAPTER 14

England Carries Off the Asses

On a tour of Australia, the England cricket team developed an exciting new approach to bowling.

They had come to realise that the game of cricket had one serious flaw. The bails were much too small to hit without a very great deal of effort, particularly if an Australian batsman was standing in the way. From now on, they would bowl the ball straight at the head of the batsman.

If by any chance the batsman's head fell off, the England team would politely ask the umpire for it to be counted as a wicket. If, on the other hand, the batsman's head merely spun round and round, the England team would do the decent thing, and give him another go.

Being unEnglish, the Australian team vociferously accused the England XI of not playing fair. But the English umpire said he couldn't understand a word they were saying so England once again walked away with the Asses.

The Harrow Crusade

In 1936, hundreds of Harrow pupils were suffering from depression so they marched barefoot into the centre of London. They were protesting against being the poor cousins of Eton.

On their long march south, the Harrow Crusade gained

23

a great deal of public sympathy. To keep them going, ordinary decent Britons dangled out of upstairs windows, tossing them nutritious scraps of used cabbage.

But Prime Minister Stanley Boredom was having none of it. 'The voice of the Harrow Marchers must be heard', he told a packed House of Commons. But the Etonians to whom the speech was addressed could not hear it. They were all in the House of Lords.

CHAPTER 15

Stirring Up Inaction

Mahatma Grandhi walked around India in his loincloth and Nehru jacket stirring up inaction. He advocated a new form of passive resistance, to be known as a pacifistfight. An extraordinary mixture of rebel and conformist, at formal dinners Gandhi would insist on a cut-glass decanter of his own urine being passed round the table from left to right. His boisterous wife Goosey Gandhi had an affair with Lord Louis Mountbottom. This served only to increase popular demand for partitions. Gandhi later put on ten stone to play the title role in *Dikhi*, the award-winning film based on the life of Lord Attenborough.

A Telephone Rings

By the mid-1930s, the people of Britain were growing used to the telephone. Many telephones were sold after they had been invented by Alexander Gissa Bell, but few Britons knew how to use them. This meant that for years telephones could be heard ringing in houses, but no one knew what on earth it meant. Years later they discovered how to lift the receiver, but it turned out to be a wrong number.

Hollywood Stars Lack Character

In the 1930s, America attempted to take over from Britain as the film capital of the world, but with no success. While the stars of Pinewood and Ealing remained themselves and refused to show off, Hollywood stars were notoriously difficult and insisted on acting.

Many British actors gained knighthoods, grew moustaches and took up responsible jobs. The same cannot be said of

Hollywood stars, who would invariably embark upon a cycle of decline, and be driven to drink.

Film historian David Thomson writes:

Mickey Mouse was a virtual unknown when he was cast by Walt Disney to star in his first feature film in 1928. He rapidly became the biggest movie star the world had ever known. But fame took its toll. Yes, he seemed to have everything – but did Mickey Mouse ever know who he really was?

Inevitably his fans soon deserted Mickey for ducks, coyotes and even dwarfs. Mickey tried everything to win them back, including elocution and extensive ear surgery.

Worried that he was becoming type-cast, he changed his name to Michael J. Mouse and accepted only a small wage to star in a *film noir* directed by Fritz Fang called Mouse of Horror. But it was a whisker that failed to pay off. His fans refused to accept him as a serious actor. Before the end of the decade, Mickey began to binge on Stilton, Cheddar and even Gorgonzola.

By this time, he had split up with his glamorous young starlet bride, Minnie, who was now being seen around town with his rival Grumpy, one of the Seven Dwarfs. Minnie married Grumpy in 1932, but later divorced him, claiming he had never once thanked her for anything.

Mickey Mouse was caught in a trap from which he never truly escaped. As an old mouse, he could be seen in Los Angeles' bars, bragging of the good old days when he had arm-wrestled Earnest Humaway in a Mexican bordello.

He appeared on *The Oprah Show* ('Coming to Terms with Failure') in the mid-Seventies. His last appearance was a cameo as an elderly mouse squashed to death in a car chase in *Starsky and Hutch* (1978). Mouse died of an alcohol-related illness in 1979.

The Serviette Union

Leading ineffectuals, such as playwright George Shernard Bore, Lady Aspidistra, and the Webbs, Donald and Daffy, all visited the Serviette Union in the 1930s to see how commuting worked in practice.

They returned to Britain impressed by the way Josef Stalin had arranged the table settings, adding fresh vigour and imagination to the shaping of serviettes into all sorts of exciting swan and hat arrangements so that others might be allowed to starve of their own accord.

'If I had to choose between laying a table for my friend or for my country, I would get the college servant to do both,' said Dr E. M. Forster of Gloucester, before stepping into a puddle.

CHAPTER 16

The Real Mrs Simpson

While King George V was busy with his stamp collection, his eldest son, the Prince of Wails, was dancing in all the top nightspots.

On a visit to the coalpits of South Wales, he was convinced that the people had 'blacked up' to form a minstrel band in his honour. In return, he said, 'Something must be slum, slum, slum!' before dancing the Cha-cha-cha.

Back at Sandringham, King George V's wife drew peacefully on his clothes.

Meanwhile, their elder son, the Prince of Wails, was busy dating Mrs Marge Simpson. Mrs Simpson harboured a guilty secret. Unbeknownst to anyone, she was an American. Born Bessie Wallis Warfield in Baltimore, she spent the first ten years of her life as a cow, dancing the Polka on the great prairies of Alabama. But Bessie Wallis would never be satisfied with life as a cow. For her, it was time to moove on, regardless of the udders.

After pursuing her Gap Year in a high-class brothel in Hong Kong, and enjoying a season as a pantomime cow at the Theatre Royal, Windsor, she changed her name to Marge Simpson and got married on a regular basis. But one day at a dinner party in England she was introduced to the Prince of Wails.

Mrs Simpson was not only very backward, she was also very forward. When the Prince of Wails asked her, 'And what do you do?' she replied, 'I am busy capturing the heart of a man who will give up his throne for me and then we will live together in exile, pursuing an empty lifestyle.'

Unprepared for this backwardly forward American way of talking, the Prince of Wails was bowled off his feet. He instantly blew hot and cold on his old girlfriend, Lady Furnace, and asked Marje to marry him.

Ordinary, decent Britons were unaware that the Prince of Wails had been secretly dating Mrs Simpson. They were prevented from finding out by the Establishment, who loved keeping things secret. Down the years, authorised biographies of earlier Kings had been titled, *King Alfred and the Perfect Cakes*, *King Ethelred the Ready* and *The Wife of Henry VIII*.

Clothes Popularised by the Duke of Windsor

(a) *Windsor Change*

The Windsor Change consisted of loud plus-fours. Even the Prime Minister woke up to the Windsor Change. He said the Windsor Change were blowing loudly all over Africa.

(b) *Windsor Wore*

Headlines were made from what Windsor wore. The Duke and Duke of Windsor spent up to five hours a day tying their ties with the Windsor Knot, and another five trying to undo them.

(c) *Brown Windsor Suit*

The Brown Windsor Suit was sewn together largely from leftovers and was warm and highly nutritious.

'Something must be spun' – to the Needlewomen's Guild, 1934

'Something must be run' – at the Berlin Olympics, 1936

'Something must be fun' – Abdictation Speech, 1936

'Something must be sun' – Inaugural Speech as Governor of Bermuda, 1943

CHAPTER 17

The 1936 Olympics

In Germany, the young moustachioed landscape painter had put away his easel to give himself more time for world domination. Adolf Hitler was furious when Jessie Matthews won the

1936 Olympics. It proved that a down-to-earth British actress could beat the best Nazi athletes, armed with nothing but a cheery smile.

Hitler had put all of his plans for the 1936 Olympics in his famous Will. *The Trumping of the Will* was later filmed by three famous directors, Lenny, Griff and Stoll.

The Spanish Civil War

The Spanish Civil War took place between (a) General Frankie Vaughan, the Spanish Florist leader and (b) a small but prestigious group of English and American authors.

The authors included Earnest Humaway, author of *For Whom the Kettle Boils*. Humaway was interested in bulls and petit-point, but not necessarily in that order.

The British writers W. H. Maud, Sir Spender and Cecil Day-Return also formed a battalion to fight against the Florists, but they thought the best tactic was to lie low in a trench just north of Hyde Park.

Other English writers determined to fight against Frankie Vaughan included a detachment of the Bloomsbury Grope. They arrived in a tank driven by Vita Shredded-Wheat, directed by Virginia Woof and designed in lovely greens, pinks and mauves by Duncan Grunt, with gunner Dame Edith Spitwell taking it up the rear.

In her memorable Drearies of the period, Virginia Woof records how hectic life could be on the Front. They included upsetting passages showing the turmoil it created in one's social life:

31

Oh dear, oh dear, the lack of any proper changing facilities, the dreadful self-pitying moans and groans of the perfectly ghastly little Spanish people as their heads are blown clean awf, the higgledy-piggledy approach to laundry, the utter but utter impossibility of finding decent service in a tank.

The Left Book Club

The Left Book Club was founded to counteract the growing threat from Florism. It published books with titles like *Betrayal of the Left*, *The Road to the Left*, *Forward With the Left*, and *Signalling Left*. They were available to purchase from all good bookshops. But most of them were Left.

A New Leader

The Labour Party elected Mr Clement Hatley as its new leader. Some Labour politicians wore hats, others moustaches. But it was Mr Hatley's genius to wear both at the same time, thus securing him the leadership.

Not to be outdone, the Conservative Party searched around for someone who could take him on. Finally they appointed Mr Chambermaid, who sported not only a hat and moustache, but also a silver watch-chain. With all these things in his favour, it was thought he was the man with the apparatus to counteract the Growth of Florism, led in England by Sir Oswald, mostly.

The Birth of Monotony

In the 1930s, family life was split in two by the advent of a new bored game called Monotony. Millions of copies were sold. Families who had not spoken to each other for months would play it, and then not speak to one another for years.

CHAPTER 18

The Abdictation

Seated alone in Windsor Castle, King Edward VIII abdictated by radio to his subjects at home and abroad. 'I have found it impossible to carry the heavy burden of the woman I love,' he said, with great dignity. It all went to show that constitutional crises were what we British did best.

The unhappy couple were then bundled into the boot of a passing car and exhaled to France. They spent the rest of their lives trying on new clothes and putting a brave face on things.

King Edward VIII was succeeded by his shy brother, King George the Sick. King George the Sick had a very bad stammer. It took him five days to consent to be the new king, and a further fortnight to consent to be King George the Sick.

King George the Sick was so shy that he only agreed to go out on the balcony of Buckingham Palace if the crowds promised not to look.

By coincidence, King George the Sick married the

Queen Mother, although at that time she insisted on being called by her first name so she was just known as the Queen.

She immediately became the wealthiest and best-loved woman in the world, Empress of India and ruler of the British Empire. She never forgave Mrs Marge Simpson for all this, and only extended the hand of friendship once she was sure she was dead.

The Growing Threat from International Florism

The Prime Minister, Mr Chambermaid, was deeply concerned by the growth of the Florist Movement, so he flew over to Munich to meet their Furrier, Herr Hitler, and his fellow Florists.

These were:

Herr Dresser
Herr Stylist
Herr Wash
Herr Cutt
Herr Pin-Bend
Herr Baceous-Border

Herr Baceous-Border always planted himself at a regular distance of six inches from the others.

In return for promising to be more patient in future, Herr Hitler was allowed to keep the land he had gone to all the trouble of invading.

Mr Chambermaid arrived back home to a tumultuous welcome. It was a major diplomatic coup for Britain: in exchange for not giving Herr Hitler everything he wanted, Mr Chambermaid agreed to give him everything he had planned.

Herr Hitler had been over-awed by Mr Chambermaid's hat, his moustache and his watch-on-a-chain, so had agreed to every last one of his demands, apart from those that interfered with everything he wanted to do.

Historians now suggest that far from being a neville man, Mr Chambermaid was simply too trusting.

Upon landing at Heston service station at lunchtime, Mr Chambermaid declared, 'This morning I had another talk with the German Chancellor, Herr Hitler, and I gave him a blank piece of paper.' He then waved his menu in the air, ordering, 'Peas in an hour's time.'

This proved that Britain not only ruled the waves, but also waived the rules.

At that very moment, Yorkshire batsman Henrietta ('Hen') Lutton scored 364 runs in the final Test, ensuring that England beat Australia by an unprecedented margin of 579.

It all went to show that the British Empire was still going strong and there was nothing whatever to worry about.

The Birth of Television

Nearly seven thousand people queued at Olympia to witness the first-ever talking pictures on television. The television took a few minutes to warm up, and then the Chairman of the BBC spent another half-hour tuning it in.

Lord Wreath eventually found something worth watching, but the first-ever programme on television was greeted by moans of disappointment from the expectant crowd: it was a repeat.

CHAPTER 19

Murder in the 1930s

Murders in the 1930s were carried out in tweed suits and ties by well-respected doctors with moustaches and difficult wives.

Their medical presence ensured that the difficult task of murder was performed hygienically, and under the strictest supervision.

The corpses were then cut into neat pieces, packed into trunks and deposited in the left-luggage lockers of all the major railway termini. If ever the doctors were arrested and taken to task, they would point out in court that they had been driven to it by their difficult wives. The judges would then tell them to say sorry nicely.

Ordinary decent Britons today look back on this period as a golden age, a time when murderers had impeccable manners, well-brushed hair and decent jobs.

Since then, things have gone downhill. Nowadays when members of the public visit the Chamber of Horrors at Madame Tussaud's, they like to recall a time when men's tailoring was at its height, and every doctor knew how to maintain a tidy trunk.

Arts in the Thirties: the Sitford Misters

On the Continent, foreigners had to make do with Picasso, Cocteau, Shostakovich and Matisse. But Britain could boast the Sitford Misters.

Their father, a lord, was called Farv, while their mother, a commoner, was called Parv. They also had a less well-known brother, a midget called Harv, an anorexic maid called Starv, a chef called Carv, and a common handyman called Chav.

This remarkable family, always right at the very forefront of British national life, included:

- Decca, the recording artiste
- Pecca, the nymphomaniac
- Recca, the anarchist
- Becca, the Wimbledon champion
- Mecca, the Islamic fundamentalist.

Appeasoupers

The Appeasoupers were the fashionable group of foggy thinkers who supped on pea soup served by a tight-lipped butler played by Anthony Hopkins. They gathered in Lord Astor La Vista's stately home outside Halifax, where they entertained the more fashionable Nazis, such as Rob and Viv Tropp.

CHAPTER 20

The State of Empire

The Queen Mother was the last Queen of an Empire on which the sun never set.

And, in time, her grandson would come to inherit an island over which *The Sun* never set.

CHAPTER 21

The War to End Peace

The British Ambassador in Berlin handed the German government a final note asking for an undertaking by elevenses that in the unlikely event of a war:

1. It should be made quite clear exactly whose side everyone was on.
2. It wouldn't go on too long.
3. Clear arrows should be painted on all maps showing troop advances, etc., so that everyone could understand who was doing what, where and to whom.
4. England should be allowed to win easily.

5. In the long run, it might be best for world peace if Herr Hitler had another go at painting. His sunsets really do show promise.

6. A list of the five causes of the Second World War should be handed out to everyone immediately after it had finished.

But towards the end of elevenses, an ashen-faced Mr Chambermaid announced, 'I have to tell you now that no such undertaking has been received, and that consequently this country is at war with Germany. I could murder a biscuit.'

TEST PAPER II

The Thirties

The sauces in this question paper have been reduced to make them easier to pour over.

THE SPANISH CIVIL WAR
Coursework Assignment

1 (a) Whose side was Franco on in the Franco-Prussian war?
   (b) Why was the Spanish War considered civil?
   (c) Who signed the King of Spain's beard?
   (d) Or is that the wrong war?

2 Tick in a box:

   (f) Answer this question without reference to any THREE of

the following: Don Quixote, castanets, matadors, Spanish Harlem, *The Barber of Seville*, flamenco.

(g) 'The rain in Spain falls mainly on the hilly bits.' True or false?

(h) Mussolini and Franco were roughly the same person. If not, why not?

3 Once you have finished reading this question, insert it in a box, then tick it.

THE ABDICATION CRISIS

Study Sauces A to C, then question ALL the answers.

Use the sauces and then consume the Topic in your own time.

Sauce A: A photograph of the wedding of the Duke and Duchess of Windsor.

Sauce B: A photograph of the Duke and Duchess of Windsor as the Ugly Sisters in the pantomime *Cinderella* at the Bristol Hippodrome in 1961.

Sauce C: A souvenir tea-towel showing the Queen Mother waving at well-wishers from the balcony of Clarence House, 1961

Imagine you are the Duchess of Windsor. It is the day after your wedding. You have just unwrapped your present from your new

sister-in-law, Queen Elizabeth. It is a packet of six paper serviettes. One has already been soiled. Describe how you feel.

5   What happened to Question 4? Give reasons.

6   Either: You are a member of the Bloomsbury Grope. You
    don't feel like playing tennis, as your beard always gets in the
    way. Could you be persuaded to play a throwing game using
    a spherical object? Discus.

    Or: Did Virginia Woof influence Hitler's decision to invade
    Russia? If not, why not? Write the answer on the back of
    your hand.

7   MURDER IN 1930S
    (i)   If it takes one man 38 minutes to cut up a corpse and
          pack it into a trunk, and the same man 12 minutes to
          book the trunk into Left Luggage at Victoria Station,
          how long would it take three men to cut up and book
          in five corpses, if two of them were doctors?
    (ii) Describe, with diagrams where necessary, Adolf Hitler's
          involvement in the Brighton Trunk Murders.

Turn over the page.
    Now turn it over again.
    You are back to where you were before.

8   CHAMBERMAID
    (a)   Remind me again, but where exactly did Halifax fit in?
    (b)   How was Halifax building society?

9 Explain the five causes of this question employing diagrams where necessary.

THE FORTIES

A Decade of Storms and Clouds

In a very real way, the 1940s may be said to have divided the 1930s from the 1950s. Historians are agreed that without the 1940s, there could have been no 1950s.

It is a decade of turmoil and chaos. The stormclouds gather, then burst, then gather, then burst, only to gather again, then burst again. It is a process that is to be repeated many times before the decade is out.

CHAPTER 22

The Nazi War Machine

The Nazi War Machine consisted of:

(i) *Pansy Divisions*
Hitler formed several Pansy Divisions from blond-haired young men in uniform and leather boots. They were the very cream of his proposed Fairyan nation, and

"GET U BOAT!"

would surprise their enemies by ambushing them with 'Tomorrow Belongs To Me', 'Come to the Cabaraaaaaay' and other favourites by Liza Minnelli.

(ii) *U-Boats*

These boats were designed to travel in a U direction. This proved a tactical error, as no sooner had they set off than they would be back.

(iii) *Hit-a-Youth Movement*

To encourage the war effort, Hitler formed the 'Hit-a-Youth' movement. Fresh-faced youths, brimful of confidence, would line up to be hit by their elders and betters.

(iv) *The Dessert Fats*

Many Nazi leaders suffered from severe weight gain, owing to a penchant for puddings. They were known as the Dessert Fats, a crack squadron of the clinically obese, capable of demolishing a dessert in a matter of minutes. The Dessert Fats were led by Herman Groaning and a group of volauventeers.

(v) *Lord Haw-Haw*

Lord Haw-Haw (see Crazy Paving) was the real name of Dublin-born James Joyce who, with his wife Yootha (see Hitler Yootha), would broadcast lengthy stream-of-consciousness sections of his book *Useless* from a secret outpost in Berlin, hoping to sow the seeds of discontent in the English-speaking world.

(vi) *The Waffle SOS*

Under the direct command of Heinrich Dimmler-und-Dimmler, the Waffle SOS was a crack squadron specially formed to get into tight spots before sending out wordy messages begging for help.

(vii) *The Afrika Korps*

A krakk-squadron specially formed to kleanse the letter
C from any klauses in which it kropped up. For a
konsiderable time, the Korps aktually sukkeeded in its
kampaign to enkirkle enemy kombatants, but inkorrekt
taktiks in unkonventional klimates kaused it to kollapse,
and by the klose of kombat it faked dekimation.

(viii) *The Messy Schmidts*

A group of Nazi aviators who refused to wash before
battle. This created a deathly smell everywhere, particularly in their cockpits.

The British War Effort

Unlike the Nazis, the British did not have a War Machine.
We had a War Effort. The British War Effort consisted of:

(i) *The salt of the earth*

The ordinary British Tommy went into battle puffing
on a Capstan, whistling a merry tune and making
thumbs-up signs at his chums. His pluck and good cheer
proved more than a match for the sour-faced underhand
Nazis, who were forced to rely on weaponry.

(ii) *The Home Guard*

Armed with nothing more than a nice leg of lamb and
a garden hoe, young and old alike prepared to do battle
with the Nazi War Machine by turning all the signposts
round and placing sprigs of fern in their helmets.

(iii) *Officers disguised as Frenchmen*

The average British officer spent the war behind the lines disguised as a Frenchman, wearing nothing but a black beret and a string of onions to distract attention from himself.

(iv) *Code-busters in specs*

At Bitchily and Tetchily Park, highly strung men and women in thick spectacles sat stooped over crossword puzzles and chessboards in chilly, poorly lit rooms throughout the night attempting to catch the famous Enigma cold.

(v) *The RAF*

'Prangs away!'; 'Get weaving, Burton!'; 'My chocs are going for a shaky-do!' Throughout the war, the Nazi War Machine occupied its time trying to decipher what on earth the RAF were saying to one another. It turned out that no one in the RAF had the foggiest idea: talking nonsense to one another is what we British do best.

(vi) *Steve McQueen*

Though often thought of as an American, Steve McQueen was, of course, English.

CHAPTER 23

A Memorable Broadcast

After the Battle of Britain, Winston Churchill appeared on the *Today* programme on the BBC Home Service to broadcast to the nation:

MR CHURCHILL: Never in the field of—

INTERVIEWER: When you say never, Mr Churchill—

MR CHURCHILL: Never in the—

INTERVIEWER: If I could just stop you there, Mr Churchill—

MR CHURCHILL: Never in the field of human conflict was so much owed—

INTERVIEWER: You say so much is owed, well – ha! – perhaps you could give our listeners some idea about when it is going to be paid back—

MR CHURCHILL: – was so much owed by so many—

INTERVIEWER: So what you're really saying – and correct me if I'm wrong, Mr Churchill – is that, frankly, you haven't got the foggiest!

MR CHURCHILL: – by so many to so—

INTERVIEWER: I'm sorry, that's all we've got time for.

The Berlitz

For a year, the Nazi War Machine bombarded London with *Teach Yourself German* pamphlets. This period came to be known as the Berlitz.

Throughout the war, communication proved a problem. Confronted by a British Tommy, German soldiers would invariably panic and scream nonsense, forcing the British Tommy to reach for his dictionary.

Some Useful Phrases

Achtung! Schweinhund!: I'm acting the giddy goat!
Donner und blitzen!: Give me a reindeer!

Gott in kummel!: Can I offer you a fancy liqueur?
Schnell! Schnell!: I smell a smell!
Hande hoch!: Hand over your hog!
Sprechen sie Deutsch?: Have you broken the deck-chair?
Kommen sie hier!: They're a bit common here.

CHAPTER 24

A Conspiracy

On an ill-fated mission to secure peace in 1941, Adolf Hitler's second-in-command, Dame Rudolf Hess, secretly flew to Britain armed only with a grand piano to perform a series of clandestine lunchtime concerts at the National Gallery.

After the war, Dame Rudolf was imprisoned from top to toe in Spandex, ready to start a new career as a much-loved conspiracy theory, jointly assassinating President Kennedy in 1963, before going to ground in Loch Ness.

The French Resistance

To avoid detection, the French resisted the Nazi jackboot in absolute secret. Even by the end of the war the Nazis still had absolutely no clue that they had been so busy resisting.

With the defeat of the Nazis, it fast emerged that the entire French nation had been bravely resisting all along. Under the brilliant guise of collaboration, ordinary men and women had performed well-disguised acts of resistance, such as entertaining Nazi stormtroopers in their homes and turning in Jews.

Brilliantly disguised acts of vandalism against the invaders included:

(i) *Hurling the Onion*

Using a stop-watch, a member of the Resistance would wait ten minutes after a Nazi battalion had marched past. Then, quick as a flash, he would get out a knife, cut up an onion and throw it into his evening soup in defiance.

(ii) *Whistling 'La Marseillaise'*

Many brave Frenchmen stood to attention in the middle of busy streets and whistled 'La Marseillaise'. For maximum impact, they chose to do this in the summer of 1946.

(iii) *Wearing stripy shirts and berets*

Only after the war did it emerge that every Frenchman who had bravely worn a stripy shirt and beret during the Occupation was in fact a secret member of the Resistance.

Viv la France

Those against the Germans were known as the Three French. The leader of the Three French was General de Girl. Together with his partner Viv la France, he outsmarted the Nazis by remaining in Britain while they were in France, then returned in triumph the second they left, his chest heaving with brightly coloured new medals he had bravely pinned on himself without a thought for his own safety.

CHAPTER 25

The Greater Scrape

The Nazis hit upon the devilish plan of locking up all the pluckiest British escapers in a castle full of secret passages and hidden doorways. They permitted them nothing but a selection of ropes, false passports, fancy moustaches and German phrase-books, a full range of pantomime costumes, a wooden horse, a catapult, a motorbike, a couple of gliders and a variety of buckets and spades. Before long, hundreds of British officers were burrowing their way into the castle to spend six months plotting their escape.

Five British War Heroes

1. *Lord Louis Mountbottom*

   Louis Mountbottom led many daring naval escapades, yet never messed up his perfect creases. However hard the Nazi War Machine plotted to ruin Mountbottom's tailoring, the Royal Navy always managed to outwit them by veering off to one side. This led him to a starring role in the wartime film *In Which We Swerve*.

2. *Dame Vera Drake*

   Known as the Forces' Sweetheart, Dame Vera Drake promised ordinary Tommies that when they arrived back at Dover Cliff would be there to greet them with a medley of his favourite hits. As a result, they stayed away; many still blame Dame Vera for prolonging the war.

3. *General Montgomery*

   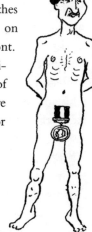

   Better known as the Full Monty, owing to his habit of appearing without any clothes to boost morale. Montgomery fought on many fronts, but principally the Y-front. Monty mistrusted Patton, who was suspicious of Auchinleck, who was wary of Mountbottom, who wasn't entirely sure of Alan Brooke, who had little time for Bummer Harris, who distrusted Monty.

4. *Legless Larder*

   Commemorated in the film *Reach for the Pie*, Legless Larder made repeated night-time raids on the Nazi food-piles.

5. *Colonel Bogey*

   Colonel Bogey was famous for whistling jaunty tunes. He was furious when someone blew up his favourite bridge, calling them 'Damn busters'.

Churchill: Further Reading

The Winston Who Knew Me

In this magisterial work, former Conservative leader Margaret Thatcher shows Churchill as a pioneering monetarist, with no need for sleep and a heartfelt desire to keep Britain out of Europe.

Churchill and My Own Good Self

In this magisterial work, former SDP leader Joy Renkins shows Churchill as a pioneering social democrat, with a penchant for fine claret and a heartfelt desire to see Britain right at the very heart of Europe.

Churchill the Canadian

In this magisterial work, former mogul Conrad Black shows Churchill as a pioneering Canadian, with an expanding newspaper empire and a heartfelt desire to keep out of prison.

Churchill the Ballerina

In this magisterial work of parallel history, former historian Andrew Roberts wonders what might have happened had Winston Churchill turned his back on the war and pursued a career as a prima ballerina.

Three Memorable British Spies

1. *Boodle, Doug*
   The famous Doug Boodle, or Bouncing Bum, was regularly dropped on enemy forces, making a whining sound as he sailed through the air, prior to bouncing.
2. *Pearl Harbor*
   The brilliant double-agent and sex-temptress who managed to infiltrate enemy lines and seduce the entire American nation into joining in.
3. *Martyr Harry*
   Harry self-sacrificingly agreed to dress up as an Eastern Temptress and sing to portly Nazi generals in the nightclubs of Europe.

The Royal Family at War

The Royal Family spent the war sitting in a bath with three inches of water, eating nothing but pork luncheon meat. On hearing news of the East End, the Queen Mother expressed shock that it should be there and vowed to pay it a visit at her earliest convenience.

The Duke and Duchess of Windsor spent the war in Bermuda Shorts, attending to those of their friends who had recently been murdered by one another.

On Gracie Fields

'And now we lie on Gracie Fields,' wrote the poet, summing up every young man's dream.

Gracie Fields, or 'Our W.G. Gracie', was popularly known as the Forces' Sweetbread. Yet her long beard struck terror into the very heart of the enemy. The moment she spotted enemy aircraft overhead, she would start swinging her bat and singing. 'The Biggest Aspidistra in the World' at the top of her voice. Enemy aircraft would instantly scatter, and the 'all clear' would be sounded.

CHAPTER 26

Four Memorable Nazis: One Bad, One Good, One Not Quite So Good, and One with Lovely Manners

1 *Josef Gerbil*

In a surprise move, Hitler made his pet Gerbil head of propaganda. From his wheel on the front line, Gerbil became the master of spin.

2. *The Desert Fax*

General Rommel was nicknamed the Desert Fax. This was because he was always slipping in somewhere and slipping out somewhere else, often suffering a breakdown in the process. Unlike all the others, the Desert Fax was a Good German, who didn't really want to fight but couldn't think of anything better to do.

3. *Admiral Duncan Dönitz*

Was Duncan Dönitz a Good German? Most historians are now agreed that, when all is said and done, he was an Only Quite Good German.

Most of the time, he was away at sea, so had no idea there was a war on. The first he heard of it was when news reached him that Hitler had just appointed him his successor as Supreme Head of the Third Reich. Dönitz was delighted. Only later did he come to realise there might be a catch in it somewhere.

4. *Albert Square*

Square was the most eminently civilised of all Hitler's henchmen. He had beautiful manners, and lovely clean nails. The English took him to their heart.

Albert Square favoured architecture on a grand scale. His first design was for a loft conversion based on the Colosseum in Rome. His second design, a shoebox, held over 100,000 shoes. It took 100 men 200 days to find a pair that matched.

Poor Albert only found out he was a Nazi in the last few days of the war, when it was far too late to do anything about it.

He later confessed to having no idea that the man he worked for was in charge of the Nazi War Machine. 'Of course, one knew Adolf had a hectic lifestyle,' he confessed, 'but if only one had twigged he was Führer!'

At the Nuremberg Trials, the judges took his lovely manners into account. They were particularly impressed by the way he confessed to everything. They took it as clear proof of his innocence.

55

They reluctantly sentenced him to a few years in Spandau Ballet with Dame Myra Hess, to be served on his own convenience.

CHAPTER 27

Rationing in War

Food in wartime was strictly rationed. This led to many enterprising recipes, with all the available ingredients put to imaginative use. One particular favourite involved mixing Powdered Egg with Spam and Bully Beef. This produced Bully Egg Powdered Spam Beef, and ensured no one took more than their fair share.

Luxury items such as ice-cream remained in short supply. Housewives were forced to improvise by making it from the superfluous limbs of household pets – hence the famous wartime expression 'Walls Have Ears'.

Three Memorable Wartime Songs

'Whale Meat Again'
Wartime food rationing inspired this memorable wartime song by Dame Vera Drake.

'In A Mood'
Temperamental wartime bandleader Glenn Miller was famous for his mood-swings, which emerged in his signature Big

Bland Sound. 'In A Mood' was one of his most famous songs. It was sung by Moonlight Sarah Nade.

'My Little Ukelelelele'
George Formby did his bit to keep the enemy at bay during the Blitz by strumming on his little ukelelelele and singing in his high-pitched voice.

Entertainment in the War

Families would gather round the wireless in their air-raid shelters to hear Professor Toad put on his thinking cap and tackle such questions as 'Is there a God?'

He would reply, 'It all depends what you mean by "God". Next question, please.' Professor Toad was later arrested for not having a railway ticket. This became known as the Trains Bust.

On the silver screen, Laurence of Olivier re-enacted his epic Henry V on his trademark camel. One of the big wartime hits was Trevor Howard and Celia Johnson in their stiff-upper-lip romantic weepie *Briefs Counted*.

Bridge on the River Kwai

The stiff upper lip of the British soldier was tested almost to breaking point with regular afternoon sessions of bridge on the River Kwai between Colonel Bogey and the ridiculous Japanese leader Lord Haw-Haw.

Artists and War

Many artists did their bit for the war effort by fearlessly flying to America. By registering their protest so sensitively they sought to force Adolf Hitler to see the error of his brutal ways.

Among those who wished to strike terror into the Nazis by leaving England were Benjamin Bitten, composer of *Anyone for Venice*; his friends Peter Groans and Billy Bunter; the poet W. H. Maud, and Christopher Hollywood, author of *Goodbye to Bowls*, starring Sally Berlin.

CHAPTER 28

Two Notable Contributions

The Russians

Reputable English historians now claim that the Russians also fought in the Second World War. But they didn't really count, as they refused to be led by proper English Generals. Instead, they opted for Russian Generals with names far too long to be taken seriously. So they have only themselves to blame if their contribution is overlooked.

The Americans

The Americans stepped into the war at the last moment, just as everyone was packing up. They then re-shot it using their own actors, first as World War, then as World War 2, then as World War 2: The Sequel.

10 Memorable Wartime Days

1. VE Day
2. VJ Day
3. PJ Day
4. V-Neck Day
5. VIP Day
6. D Day
7. VD Day
8. Doris Day
9. Day-oh
10. Day-ay-ay-oh

CHAPTER 29

Hitler's Final Days

A keen golfer, Hitler spent his last days in a bunker, attempting one last great drive.

With his fiancée, Eva Brick, and Gerbil he put on a brave face. On being told that Germany was in ruins and the Allied troops were within spitting distance, he sighed impatiently. 'Okay,' he snapped. 'Let's start again from scratch – but this time let's get it right.'

His wedding in the bunker to Eva Brick went as smoothly as could be expected. But their honeymoon was postponed due to unforeseen circumstances. The bride wore white; the groom wore a scowl. The throwing of confetti was not permitted, to avoid making a mess outside the bunker. A selection of cyanide-based nibbles was handed around at the reception; a few hours later, the newly-weds went off with a bang.

CHAPTER 30

The Stormclouds Depart

The announcement that the war was at an end inspired unprotected dancing with strangers in the streets; within minutes, everyone became pregnant.

Meanwhile, the Royal Family appeared on the balcony of Buckingham Palace in their bath eating bananas on behalf of the nation.

Londoners cheered them for being the only Royal Family in the world to have lived in Buckingham Palace throughout the war. The Queen Mother took the opportunity to scan London with her racing binoculars for any sign of the East End.

Down below in the Mall, ordinary decent Britons danced cheek-to-cheek to 'Knees Up Miss Brown' (previously 'Knees Together, Miss Brown') and 'Hokey Cokey' by Focus before giving birth to hippies.

CHAPTER 31

Nothing Happens

Everyone was so completely exhausted after winning the war that for some years nothing happened at all.

For the next half-decade events were available only in black and white, and strictly rationed to one per year, rising to two in 1947, but none in 1948.

1945: The Conservative Party disappears beneath a Landslide. The Labour Party steps in under Clement Hatley, a man with a moustache.

Hatley sets about creating the Farewell State, which, he explains, will serve people 'from the ladle to the gravy'.

From now on, the state will look after ordinary decent Britons until they drop dead. The state also takes over the running of railways and coal mines.

The men now in charge of everything are identical

Welsh twins called Bevin and Bevan. But no one can tell one from the other, so no one knows who to complain to.

1946: With rationing still under way, crowds flock to the Odeon, Leicester Square to enjoy a film of an American eating a banana.

1947: Princess Elizabeth marries Prince Philip. The wedding banquet consists of a dish of Spam carved into exotic shapes, with red jelly and half a tin of condensed milk to follow. Afterwards, guests gathered in the ballroom to be shown slides of a pineapple.

1947: The Empire in India is now closed due to poor attendance. The Curzon, too, has closed down, and so has the Imperial. The Vice, Roy Mountbottom, puts on his braid and dons his peaked cap to manage the closing-down ceremony. At the stroke of midnight, the main feature stops, and Mountbottom ushers out the end of an error.

1949: But at least there is some good news back in England, where an English team wins the County Championship, under the doughty English batting of Denis Competent.

It Turns Out Something Did Happen, but Only Abroad

Years later, it was discovered that something did in fact happen at this time, or a little earlier, but it had happened abroad, so it didn't really count.

It was in the region of Kenya known as Nappy Valley, an area of the Dark Incontinent.

The 22nd Earl of Errors, an alcoholic rake, was found lying on the ground with a bullet through his head. No one thought much of it at the time, but suspicions mounted after someone noticed that the Earl had been refusing his drinks for well over a week.

The police were called in when it became clear that everyone was reluctant to touch the alcoholic rake in case he bounced up unexpectedly and hit them in the face.

The mainlining suspects included:

Gwladys, Gwlady Bloodimare (*Pronounced B'are*): alcoholic seductress who was secretly seeing *Sir Jock Dinners-Broughtup* (Pronounced B'urp)

Sir Jock Dinners-Broughtup: alcoholic rake who was secretly seeing *Lady Cholmondelemondeley* (pronounced Cholmondeley).

Lady Cholmondeley: alcoholic temptress who was secretly seeing *Gwladys, Gwlady Bloodimare.*

The 22nd Earl of Errors (*Pronounced D'ead*): alcoholic aristo-crat who was secretly seeing himself after his death.

The Mau-Miaow: the Earl's vicious alcoholic tom-cat.

The 1940s

1. Refer to source A.

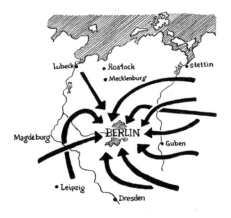

Study this map carefully before skipping the next question.

Question: In the final stages of the war, why did Adolf Hitler make the mistake of leaving so many arrows on the ground to indicate exactly where he was hiding?

2. Tick in the box
   (i) Where did Churchill announce he would fight?
      (a) in the breeches
      (b) on the speeches
      (c) over the teachers
      (d) under the lychees?

(ii) Which of these was *not* a World War 2 Commander?
   (a) Marion Montgomery
   (b) Marguerite Patton
   (c) Marshall Plan
   (d) Major Diversion

3. How did de General have de Gaulle? Give reasons.

4. Source B: Hitler in his bunker

Imagine you are Adolf Hitler. It is the morning of 30 April 1945.
   (a) How are you feeling? Unburden yourself in no more than 50 words. Do not take longer than three minutes over this question.
   (b) Ask yourself: where did it all go wrong? Give examples.
   (c) On balance, might you have better career prospects if you had stuck to being a painter?
   (d) Why didn't you make a five point plan?

5. Whatever happened to:
   The Southern Front?
   The Northern Front?
   The Cold Front?
   The Y Front?

6. 'General Auchinleck at El Alamein'. Say it 5 times very very quickly.

7. Compare and contrast (a) the Desert Rat with (b) the Desert Fox. Provide recipes for both.

8. You are the commander of a battalion. The bridge ahead has been destroyed. Devise a plan to cross Alan Brooke.

9. (i) Describe the causes of the causes of the Second World War.
   (ii) What caused them to be caused?

THE FIFTIES

The Age of Austerity

It is, above all, a decade of contrasts, the end of the old and the birth of the new.

At 10 Rillington Place, Mr John Christie is the very last full-time murderer to wear a well-cut suit and tie, with a hat to match. The suave new Prime Minister, Mr Anthony Eden, is respected for wearing a Hamburger on his head.

At the same time, there are tell-tale signs of discontent within the old order: at Aldermaston, men with pipes march in duffel coats, and the British secret service is suspected of having been infiltrated by pies.

At the Royal Court Theatre, a kitchen sink creates a dreadful scene.

CHAPTER 32

A New Elizabethan Age (1)

At the start of the Fifties, the Festival of Britain set out to show that, even if Britain had lost her Empire, she could still construct towers and pavilions that would stay more or less upright for almost a year.

Among those who helped design the Festival was Conran the Barbarian, who went on to found the Hobbit Tat empire, forcing chicken-bricks into every home. Later, Conran revealed he was the first-ever Briton to have holidayed in France. He also invented the chicken and the egg, though not necessarily in that order.

A New Elizabethan Age (2)

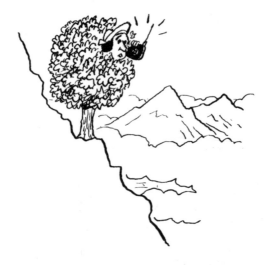

In 1952, Princess Elizabeth was halfway up a tree on Mount Everest when she heard the news of her father's death.

She hastily returned to London with her husband Prince Phlip to become Queen and usher in a new error.

The Queen's Coronation – exactly fifty years before her Golden Jubilee – took place in black-and-white, as colour was still strictly rationed. She entered the Abbey a princess; she left it Her Majesty Queen Elizabeth the Eleventh.

It was a magnificent ceremony, signalling the dawn of a new Elizabethan age: an Englishman, Sir Gordon Richards, won the Derby; another Englishman, Sir Stanley Matthews, captained an English team to victory in the FA Cup. The annual Oxford and Cambridge Boat Race was won by an English crew.

Meanwhile, an English athlete, Sir Roger Miles, became the first man to slide down a bannister in four minutes. On top of all this an Englishwoman had been made queen – and another Englishman was about to discover a vital thread.

A New Elizabethan Age (3)

That same year, Francis Crick managed to unravel D'n'A, two long twisty threads of a woolly nature, perfect for use in polo-neck jerseys and fashionable spiral staircases. Before long, everyone had their own D'n'A.

D'n'A is not to be confused with:

AND – an important conjunction
DAN – an important first name
DNB – an important work of reference
ANC – an important party
CAN – an important watering device
CND – an important campaign
CIA – an important agency
CNA – an important store.

CHAPTER 33

A Surplus of Spies

In the post-war years, most British diplomats were unmasked as Serviette spies. One of them, Guy Borges, turned out to be not only blind but South American too.

The six most important British spies were, in alphabetical order:

The Fifth Man
The First Man
The Fourth Man
The Second Man
The Sixth Man
The Third Man

Many have never been identified. However, we now know that the First Man was Neil Armstrong, and the Third Man was Orson Welles. His mask was blown by the zither music that accompanied him everywhere.

The Second Man was Guy Borges, but he kept thinking he was the Fourth and Fifth Man, because he drank too much.

The Second Man was in fact the Sixth Man, and the Sixth Man was the Second. Together they formed the Eighth Man, who has yet to be unmasked, but whom some believe to have been Dobbin, a novelty horse well known on the international pantomime circuit.

The Filth man was incorrectly identified as Mr Paul Raymond, owing to a typing error. The Eleventh Man went in last.

Princess Margaret Rose. And Fell

In 1955 Princess Margaret fell in love with Group Captain Peter Townshend, a fighter pilot with the Who, a pop group.

But it was considered Highly Unsuitable for a Princess to marry anyone who whirled about the room swinging his arm round and round, making a terrible noise. So the marriage was called off.

It seemed to many like a repeat of the Abdictation, when King Edward VIII had set his heart on marrying Mrs Marje Simpson. The match was considered Highly Unsuitable because Mr Simpson was an American. It was well known in top circles that Americans were vulgar, but Edward always denied it.

The couple changed their names to Edward and Barbara Windsor, which proved they were very vulgar after all.

CHAPTER 34

Rock Around the Crock

America's oldest man, Bill Holey, took the hit parade by storm in 1957 with his record, 'We're Going To Rock Around The Sock', causing thousands of fans to go out and buy new socks. His special new sound – known as 'crock 'n' roll' – sent thousands of future senior citizens into frenzies from which they never emerged.

The Teddy Bores

The Teddy Bores were teenaggers who spent their time swaggering around seaside resorts on scooters dressed threateningly as teddies, with slicked-back fur and knitted brows. Some rode around on mopeds. 'What did you do today?' their mothers asked. 'I just moped around,' they replied. Many came with strings attached, hoping to be pulled.

The Growth of the Teenagger

Until the mid-1950s, human beings went straight from the age of twelve to forty-three. One minute you'd be wearing shorts and playing conkers. The next you'd be striding to work in your bowler hat, a copy of the *Daily Telegraph* under your arm, fretting about your golf swing and the balance of payments deficit.

Overnight 'teenaggers' were born, upsetting everyone with their slacks and frothy coffee. They would ceaselessly nag their parents, who all lived in a circle in a square.

It was all about protest. In America, Marleen Brandy (*On the Wagon*), Jimmy Bean (*East of Anthony Eden*) and Elvis Parsley ('You Ain't Nuthin' But a Hot Dog') all broke with tradition.

After spending a night in Heartbreak Hotel, Elvis Parsley issued a protest song about the appalling service. The hotel was later refurbished, and relaunched for the more discerning traveller as the Meridien Heartbreak Hotel International.

In England, singers changed their names to reflect their new-found sense of rebellion. Marty Wilde (born Martin Milde), Billy Fury (born William Thoughtful) and Cliff Richard (born Cliff Madd) all reflected the mood of the modern teenagger.

Other aspects of the lifestyle of the teenagger included:

1. *The Duke Box*

    Old Etonians would parade into a ring in the corner of coffee-bars and box one another, taking care to stick to the Queensberry Rules. (See also *Hit Parade*).

2. *Skiffle Music*

    Wearing nothing but Terylene slacks and bootlace ties gave many teenaggers 'a slight skiffle', often with a catarrh accompaniment. Lonnie Donegan's real name was in fact Rodney Nonegan, but he could never shake off his skiffle.

5. *Rods and Knockers*

    Names given to boys and girls owing to the skin-tight trousers and sweaters they wore.

6. *Acker Bilko*

    The bowler-hatted American sergeant thrilled TV audiences with his outrageous humour and haunting clarinet.

Several Unbecoming Books

Irish novelist Nab O'Cough's *Low Litre* – about driving across America with nothing in the tank – created a sandal.

So, too, did *Lord of the Files*, about a group of boys on a desert island who try their level best to keep everything ship-shape. From America, the use of bad language in Jack Karrierbag's *One for the Road* gave rise to the term 'The Bleep Generation'. 'Dig it' was his philosophy. In a steam of conscientiousness, he set out to dig as much as possible before he needed a new Hip.

The Bleep Generation's best-known poet was Allen Ginsling, author of 'Towel!'. Ginsling encouraged people to wear towels on their heads as a protest against the Hat Race.

CHAPTER 35

The Sewers Crisis

Britain's new Prime Minister, Sir Antonia Eden, was always sensitive to smell so in 1956 she sent in troops to sort out the sewers, which were blocked. But Colonel Gnasher of Egypt didn't want them in his root canal. This created the so-called Sewers Crisis, which Britain was forced to decline.

The Sewers affair put a severe drain on Sir Antonia Eden, who ended up taking to bed with her moustaches, one on each side.

Eventually, thousands of British troops pulled out of sewers, and Colonel Gnasher was victorious.

This meant Sir Antonia proved an Unmemorable Prime Minister.

Big Mac

Who would be England's next Prime Minister? The Establishment wanted to choose a man with a moustache, so they filled a room with smoke and picked Sir Harold Macmillan, the so-called Knight of the Long Knives.

Mr Butler, who had been expecting the job, was convinced it had been stolen from him. He thus became known as 'Rob' Butler.

Harold Macmillan was popularly known as Big Mac. He spent his time as Prime Minister pushing a trolley round the world, taking everything off the shelves and supervising decline.

Big Mac was famous for cornering people in the street with his moustache, saying, 'You never had it – so long,' and beating a retreat. He was an enigma wrapped up in a moustache.

The Knight of the Long Knives became a lifelong Conservative after witnessing the disastrous effects of the General Strike. He vowed then and there that never again would a member of the upper classes be asked to drive a bus.

As Prime Minister, he made all his most important decisions on the grousemoor, shooting one grouse, or two grice. The real term for two grice is a brace, which you put in your mouth.

Big Mac always wore a top hat and tails. He spent his time counting the family silver, surrounded by Old Etonians on the one hand and grubby-faced little street urchins on the other. He didn't know what to do with them all so he put them in his One Nation Conservatory and shut the door firmly behind him.

'The wind of change,' he once said, 'is blowing from the incontinent.'

CHAPTER 36

C.U.D.

The Campaign for Unclear Disarmament was started by four celebrated pipe-smokers:

1. *J. B. Priestley*. Millions would tune in their wirelesses to hear this sensible fellow puffing on his pipe in a down-to-earth manner. They admired the way he always took care to place the narrow end matter-of-factly in his mouth.

2. *Bertrand Rissole*. The celebrated ninety-nine-year-old thinker, famous for his brilliant but flawed *History of Western Phisolophy*. Rissole, a natural rebel, preferred to smoke his pipe with the more bulbous end in his mouth. This sometimes led to smoke emerging from his ears.

3. *Canon Joan Collins*. The lissome clergyman who went on to star in such great anti-war classics as *The Sud*, set in a bath-tub, and *The Itch*, which some found irritating. Canon Joan Collins would only ever light her pipe after all other avenues had been explored.

4. *Alderman Maston*. The stuttering, pipe-smoking northern councillor famous for being marched on by his supporters at his home in Bruce, Kent.

The Angry Young Men

The Angry Young Men was the name given to a group of touchy middle-aged men. They were led by John Osbore, whose play *Look Black In Ongar*, featuring the Black and White Minstrels, was premièred at the Royal Court Theatre, Ongar, in 1956.

The first act was set in a shabby bed-sit. So was the second act. There was no scene change for the third act.

In the first act, the anti-hero shouts at the anti-heroine.

In the second act, the anti-heroine shouts back at the anti-hero.

In the third act, they shout at each other.

The kitchen sink is quiet throughout. The kitchen sink was instantly hailed as a mantelpiece by all the angriest critics of the time.

'I honestly don't think I could ever love anyone who didn't like "Oh, Mr Porter",' announced the louche critic Kenneth Tiresome.

Overnight, many more Angry Young Men emerged bearing kitchen sinks.

They included:

- **Kingsley Amis, 64.** Amis was especially angry about split infinitives, modern jazz and sloppy service in restaurants.
- **Philip Larkin, 65.** Life for Ma and Pa Larkin seemed 'perfick' before they gave birth to young Philip, who emerged as the angriest member of the Larkin Family. As a young man of 65, what made him particularly angry was overdue library books.

- **Colin Sillibraine, 63**. The author of *Lonely Sunday Morning Outside the Room at the Top*, was absolutely livid about everything in society. But then he sold the film rights, moved down south to a five-bedroomed house in Hampstead and found inner peace.
- **Arthur Askey, 73.** Celebrated for 'Buzz Buzz Buzz Buzzy Bee, Buzzy Bee', Askey has been erroneously included in lists of Angry Young Men. In fact he was always perfectly content.
- **Barbara Cartland, 65.** The famous 'Crusader in Pink', was never an angry young man.

CHAPTER 37

The Space Race

The Americans and the Serviettes attempted to make a splash with headline-grabbing projects, but Britain continued to lead the world in space exploration.

The Serviettes sent a nicked spud into space and watched it circle the earth. The Americans responded with a set-a-light rocket, launched by Eva Braun, the mastermind behind the Nazis' V8 programme. This involved shooting cartons of refreshing vegetable juice into outer space. But it was the British who invented the Bubble Car.

The Russians sent a chimp into space. In return, the Americans sent a champ into space.

Not to be outdone, the British sent a chump into space. He insisted he knew the way, but he took a wrong turning, and ran out of petrol. But no one could deny our sense of design was second to none.

The Last Debs

For sentries, every young lady called Debs had been invited to Buckingham Palace to be Presented and Caught. Traditionally, the presentation of the Debs was followed by Queen Charlotte's Bawl, a marvellous chance to meet men and get pregnant. Debs would then formally 'come out', showing the world that they were not the marrying type. But this age-old tradition ended in the 1950s, when the coming out of Debs was seen as a relic from an earlier error.

Colony Irritation

Throughout the Fifties, there was Trouble in the Colonies:

Aden: The young fifties freedom-fighter James Dean was best known for his role in *East of Aden*.

Korea: What sort of Korea opportunities were available? Korea officers were sent in to give advice. They would corner natives on street corners and demand to know, 'Are you interested in people at all – or are you better with your hands?'

Cyprus: Archbishop Macaroni led the struggle for independence in the colony of Cyprus from a hideaway beneath his beard. Macaroni pasta way in the 1970s.

Cyril Colony: The struggle against the English in the Cyril Colony is recorded in the seminal work, *The Enemies of Pommies*.

Kenya: Kenya gained its independence after a long battle against the Mau Mau, an unruly band of cats.

The Cold Ghost: The first British colony in Africa to win its independence was the Cold Ghost, better known as Mr NkruuuuumAAARGH.

CHAPTER 38

The Watershed Years

Up to the middle of the 1950s, Britain had precious few watersheds. But then there was a boom in watersheds, with a major new watershed constructed every few minutes.

Broom at the Top

For the first time in the cinema, *Broom at the Top* depicted Tony Lambton, a young upper-class rake, doing a spot of dusting with his young girlfriend. After giving his place a thorough spring-green, his girlfriend gasped, 'Oh, Tony, wasn't it supper? Wasn't it simply supper?'

This was the first time an aristocrat had ever been filmed holding a broom. Equally shocking, he was the first man to use the six-letter word 'supper' on the screen. Until then, the censor had insisted on the more socially acceptable 'dinner'.

The second man to say the word 'supper' was the critic Kenneth Tiresome.

The third man was Kim Philby.

Lady Chatterbox

A major watershed was employed by Lady Chatterbox. Lady Chatterbox frolicked in this secret love-shed with her gamekeeper, David Mellor, and a penguin.

Her husband Sir Chatterbox, a miniature car in a box, knew nothing about it. The three were prosecuted under the Seen Publications Act, charged with putting a watershed to improper use. Many distinguished figures – including Dr E. M. Forster of Gloucester and Dame Rebecca Vest – appeared on behalf of the penguin.

'You wouldn't wish to house your wife or your servant in a watershed,' said the Judge, 'or certainly not both at the same time.'

Before you could say John Robinson, Lady Chatterbox's dwelling was declared a Landmark Watershed, attracting many millions of visitors from the National Thrust.

Sicko

In the film *Sicko*, actress Janet Leigh arrives at a three-star motel. After settling in, she is stabbed to death in her watershed by Anthony Perkins, the more sinister half of the TV duo Pinky and Perkins. But, on the plus side, the room was clean and the service prompt.

The Kinky Report

In America, Dr Alfred Kinky published *The Kinky Report* after setting up a secret hidey-hole in a watershed. *The Kinky Report* discovered that a staggering 99 per cent of American males were sexually attracted to two-legged mammals. The others made do with anything they could lay their hands on.

Dulli and Bollocks

In the realm of art, Salivate Dulli, the world's leading moustache, was busy painting dream-like watersheds. He would mysteriously reverse the shed and the water to create a strange sort of shedwater.

Meanwhile, major American artist Jackson Bollocks was

throwing letters any-old-how over the canvas. This became known as Distracted Expansionism. His shaterwedswdwershatde now fetch many millions of dollars.

The 1950s

1. Why did the Coronation Chicken cross the road?

2. The Angry Young Men:

    (i) Do you (a) agree or (b) disagree with this statement?

    (ii) If you don't disagree with it, why not?

    (iii) I said, Why not? I'm not going to ask you again.

    (iv) OK. That's it. I've just about had enough. Answer me, you . . . you . . . you . . .

    (v) Yes or no?

    (vi) And what the hell do you mean by that?

3. Compare and contrast any two of the following:

    (a) Lady Chatterley's Lover

    (b) Lady Chatterley's Liver

    (c) Lady Chatterley's Loafer

    (d) Lady Chatterley's Loofah

Keep your reasons to yourself.

4. Sewers Crisis:

Where was the Garden of Eden? Was it

(i)   East of Eden
(ii) West of Eton
(iii) South of Homburg
(iv) North of Watford?

5. Compare and contrast
    (i) The Lady Avon
    (ii) The Avon Lady.
Give samples.

6. 'Winston Churchill was a good peacetime Prime Minister but a poor wartime Prime Minister.' Digress.

7. 'If Hitler had won the war, Lord Rockingham's XI would still have reached number five in the Hit Parade with "Hoots Mon" in 1958.' Discuss.

8. *Either* (i) How much is that doggie in the window? Answer to within one decimal point. *Or* (ii) Does your chewing-gum lose its flavour on the bedpost overnight? Cite reasons.

THE SIXTIES

A Decade of Loose Change

Overnight, everyone is young, cool and 'with-out', discarding first their inhibitions and then their clothes. Swinging London witnesses an explosion of the 'counter-culture' when millions of young men and women make their way to London's fashionable Carnaby Street to serve behind counters.

In politics, Enoch Scowell spots a river flowing with Tizer; in the world of the arts, Mick Jigger and Marianne Handfull unleash a Mars Bra. Meanwhile, the Royal Family spend their time keeping in touch with the British people by barbecuing kilts.

CHAPTER 39

The Arse War

Harold Macmillan was a politician with bottom. When he was returned to office in 1959, he announced, 'The Arse War is obsolete', adding 'or what the common people call "out of date".'

But in the 1960s, representatives of the assless society took the world by storm. They included:

- **Burly, David:** Cockney fashion photographer
- **Cockney, David:** modern artist from the North
- **Effings, David:** Cockney star of *Blow-Off* by Antonionionioni
- **Fingy, Albert:** northern star of *The Runniness of a Long Distance Loner*
- **Margaret, Princess:** pocket-sized cockney princess
- **Paine, Michael**: East End star of *The Duchess of Alfi*
- **Quins, Mary:** identical Cockney fashion designers
- **Stamp, Tuppenny:** Cockney actor

- **Teeth, Edward:** future former Prime Minister from the East End
- **Twiglet:** wafer-thin savoury snack from the East End

These are just some of the extraordinarily colourful Sixties characters we shall meet later in this chapter.

But scientists have now firmly established that the Fifties did not finish until some way into the Sixties, so we must wait a good few years.

The Fifties in the Sixties

The Gay Brothers

The Gay Brothers loved their mum. They only ever murdered their own, but never their own mum. They had hearts of gold and were always proud to arrange funerals for their former friends and associates.

Ronnie, Reggie and Charlie Gay were born in London's East Den, where they dressed up in smart suits, formed the Gay Gang and performed emergency dental operations free of charge.

They mixed with princesses and politicians, among them Lord Booby, a panellist on the popular wireless programme *No Questions Asked*, and Elizabeth Windsor, the busty *Carry On* star and former member of the rival Royal Family.

Their deadly rivals were the Richardsons, Meg, Jill and Sandy, who owned the Crossroads Motel in King's Oak, on the outskirts of Birmingham.

The Gays were eventually brought to justice and

sentenced to five hundred years in prison. They had all died by the turn of the century, with at least another four hundred and sixty years left to serve.

The Great Drain Robbers

In 1963, a band of armed robbers made off with a drain belonging to a Royal Male. They hid the drain in a farmhouse in Buckinghamshire. It never recovered.

The Great Drain Robbers went on the runs, among them Phil Collins, who successfully hid behind a drum kit, and Ronnie Biggs, later Bonnie Riggs, who disguised himself with a series of sex-changes and went on to write a series of successful travel books under the name of Jan Morris (later Jim Morrison).

CHAPTER 40

Affairs of State

Jack Profumo-Affair was a Vice Minister of Affairs who swam into the nubile young Christine Squealer while the two were attending a topless cocktail party in the swimming pool of Cleavage, the stately home.

Among other guests having a dip at the same time were:

- **Margaret, Duchess of Gargle**, an aristocrat
- **Ivan A. Legova**, a Serviette Spy
- **Mandy Life-Boats**, a topless hostess
- **The Legless Man**, an enigma
- **Valerie Hobnob**, an actress
- **Honey von Trapp**, a member of the legendary *Sound of Music* troupe
- **Lord Booby**, a very senior figure
- **Lord Denying**, who made a loud report.

One thing led to another: Mr Profumo-Affair and Miss Squealer ended up lying in the House as the legless man passed round nibbles in a mask. Meanwhile Margaret, Duchess of Gargle, was taken aback and afront.

'You never had it so good,' observed Mr Macmillan.

The general pubic was aghast, agog and akimbo. They had never imagined that old squares formed triangles in high circles. The elderly guests who gathered naked at Cleavage became known as the Swinging Sixties.

Until then, ordinary decent Britons didn't believe that members of the English upper classes had sex. This was a blow from which the British Empire would never recover, signalling the beginning of the end of the 1950s, which had now been going on since the mid-1940s.

An Unmemorable Prime Minister

Sensing the onset of the Sixties, the legendary Big Mac decided to make way for an older man. He chose Sir Alec Stately-Whom, an Unmemorable Prime Minister. But ordinary decent Britons soon became convinced that the Sixties were round the corner. So they elected a man in a Gannet raincoat instead.

The Hound In Your Pocket

The new Prime Minister was Harold Wilson. He was determined to uncover the whereabouts of the Sixties: he sensed they were long overdue. He declared that 'the white teat of technology' would help him discover where on earth they had got to.

He wanted Britain to lead the world in the field of silence. First, he said, more young people must be given full silence training. Second, we must keep these young silentists in the country. Third, we must apply the results of this silence research to our national production effort.

At the time, Harold Wilson was seen as a Memorable Prime Minister, though no one can remember why. He is chiefly remembered for two catchphrases. The first is 'A week is a long time in Pontefract.' This still holds true today.

The second is 'the hound in your pocket'. Many continue to wonder what he meant by it. Did he really mean to say 'the hand in your pocket'? He himself never had a hound in his pocket, though he was once spotted with a hand in someone else's.

CHAPTER 41

The Sixties Finally Get Going

By 1963, the 1950s had been going for nearly thirteen years. They might have continued for ever, but one day a wealthy entrepreneur called Albert Einstein happened to walk into a cavern in Liverpool and chanced upon the Sixties.

Standing on a stage no bigger than a shoebox were the Beatles, playing all the most famous Beatles songs, including 'Love Me Do', 'She Loves You', 'And I Love Her', 'All You

Need Is Love From Me To You', 'She Can't Buy Me Love Me Do' and 'I Feel I Want to Hold Your Hand And I Love Her From Me to All You Need Is Love Me Do'.

The news of Einstein's historic discovery soon reached London. Everyone was once again proud to be British and started to swing. They all grew their hair so that the Sixties would feel at home. The new Prime Minister was so delighted by the discovery of the Sixties that he ordered the Queen to give the Beatles their BMWs back.

But within the space of a few years, it had all gone pear-shaped. The Beatles' hair kept growing and growing, over their collars, over their backs, down their legs and into their shoes, even though at that stage they refused to wear any.

Some of the Beatles went abroad to find beards. Later albums, like *The Double Fright*, showed signs of conflict. Some said their album *Let It Brie* gave off an unfamiliar smell. Were they corrupted by money? After recording Abbey National, they broke up, citing financial differences.

When the Beatles split up it became all too clear that it was now the Seventies, so no-one felt like swinging any more.

The Sad Attire Movement

The Profumo Affair gave birth to the new Sad Attire Movement, in which brilliant young men from Oxford and Cambridge paraded in cutting-edge polo-necks in shows like *That Was Weak That Was*, presented by the young David Frostbite, who was once said to have 'risen without a face'.

The Attire Movement was centred around London's Conaby Street, home to all the very latest cutting-edge fashion designers and hairdressers such as Gore Vidal and Siegfried Sassoon. Top British designer Barbara Hulahoop opened the famous boutique Bib, specialising in wipe-clean shirts and blouses, perfect for the messy eater.

Other revolutionary Sixties clothes included:

The Mini

With two in the front and two in the back, the Mini could fit into the most cramped spaces, but looked better on those with skinny legs.

The Polar Neck

Worn by key Sixties explorers, including Anthony Armstrong-Jones (later Lord C. P. Snow) and top conductor André Pervert, the Polar Neck was designed to keep photographers and dance instructors warm in simulated arctic conditions.

The Turtle Neck

Many fashionable old people were in their Sixties in the Sixties. They had Turtle Necks, which is why they wore Polar Necks.

The Flowery Tie

Up to the 1960s, by law all men's ties had to be black or (if licensed, but even then strictly for party-wear only) a very dark grey. Until 1959, anyone caught wearing a flowery tie faced arrest and possible deportation.

The Banana

Bananas were worn knotted around the head.

Bell-bottoms

Those with bell-bottoms were probably better off wearing long dresses or, in the case of men, jackets with vents.

The Trouser Suit

At the beginning of the Sixties all women wore trousers to the Savoy Hotel and were told they couldn't come in. But by the end of the Sixties even the Queen Mother was wearing jeans and a banana to Royal Ascot.

The World Cup

In 1966, England beat West Germany 40–2 to win the World Cup.

This was the last time in history when every player in the England team was called Bobby. Their average age was fifty-three.

HOW OUR BOYS LINED UP

	Bobby Banks	
Bobby Cohen		Bobby Wilson
Bobby Stiles	Bobby Charlton	Bobby Moore
Bobby Ball	Bobby Charlton jr	Bobby Peters
	Bobby Hurst	Bobby Hunt

The announcement of victory was greeted by dancing in the street. The English were magnanimous in victory, rounding up the West German losers and placing them in detention centres, after giving them a fair trial. News of the English victory was greeted with awe and envy by all the other nations of the world. Footage of the great event was screened over and over again to cheering crowds in a major London cinema.

After so many long, hard years, foreigners were forced to recognise that England had at last regained its Empire, Leicester Square.

CHAPTER 42

Rivers of Bloop

'Like the Snowman, I seem to see a river foaming with much Tizer,' said Mr Enoch Scowell in 1968.

The Tory leader, Mr Edward Teeth, immediately condemned the speech as likely to excite facial tension, and gave him the sack. Hundreds of ordinary indecent Britons marched on the House of Commons in support of Mr Scowell.

His speech was strongly supported by the white-ring Monday Club, which favoured clubbing people to death

on Mondays. Mr Scowell later left the Tory Party to take his twin moustaches to Ulcer, but he kept in constant touch by foam.

Scowell's speech led to the foundation of the 'I'm Barking Britain' campaign, formed by ordinary working people who were determined to make Britain grate again.

CHAPTER 43

The Permissive Society

After a slow start, the Sixties were soon under way, just in time for the Seventies. It was even rumoured that the younger generation were secretly loosening their ties and removing their hats before engaging in sexual congress.

Sex, which had been strictly formal, was fast becoming casual. Some young people even claimed to be doing it for pleasure. A pop record called 'Je T'Aime (Moi Non Plus)', which is literally translated as 'I am not as tame as you are' was banned because it featured two people snoring in time to the music.

Films like Antoni Onioni's groundbreaking *Blow-Off* made all the right noises. The stage play *Oh Cauliflower!* steadfastly refused to sweep nudity under the vegetable. The producer of *Oh Cauliflower!*, ex-public schoolboy Kenneth Tiresome, became famous overnight for being the first man ever to say 'ruck' on British television.

buck	Roy Rogers
duck	Johnny Morris
luck	Michael Miles
muck	Fanny Cradock
puck	Sir John Gielgud
shuck	Ronald Reagan
tuck	William Bunter

A Midlands housewife called Mrs Mary Whitehouse began to campaign against filth on television. Some argued that she saw sex where none existed, but she strongly denied it.

Among her targets were the TV series '*Till Lust Us Do Part*, the hippie musical *Hairy!*, the Beatles' film *Magical Sexuality Tour* and the BBC *Evening Nudes*.

Drugs

In the 1950s, the only drug had been aspirin. People were forced to make their own entertainment: a game of whist, a session of ballroom dancing or a round of bingo.

But in the 1960s, drugs became freely available. Photographic evidence from the time shows people smiling: these are addicts. Drugs led to hair-growth and loss of shoes. Overnight, drug references turned up in popular songs. The

hero of the chart-topping 'Puff the Magic Dragon' was not a magic dragon at all but a drug addict. And he didn't live by the sea, but on a ring-road just north of Potters Bar.

It is a well-known fact that if you take the initial letters of the Beatles' 'Lucy in The Sky With Diamonds' it becomes clear that the song is really all about the drug Litswd.

A Mars Bra

The lead singer with the Stolen Bones, Mick Jigger, was anointed the Voice of Youth. 'You'll come to know youth,' his parents told him when he was a child – and they were right.

A former student of the LSD, Jigger assembled a pop group consisting of Bill Why, Charlie What, Cliff Richard and Brian Jones, who was already dead. For their first five years they had greatest hits, and for the next thirty-five years they played them.

In 1967, police discovered Mick Jigger tucking into a Mars Bra with his girlfriend Miss Marianne Handfull and arrested both of them. They claimed in court that Miss Handfull had been wearing nothing but a fur rug over her drugs bust.

Jigger was taken to court and charged with being in possession of Miss Handfull. A packed courtroom was informed that he was the Voice of Youth, so the Establishment was sent for.

The Establishment consisted of the Archbishop of Canterbury, the Editor of *The Times*, HM the Queen Elizabeth II, the Admiral of the Fleet, the Chairman of the MCC, the Lord Chancellor and the Keeper of the Privy Purse.

They asked Jigger what it was like to be young. He told them it was like being a butterfly on a wheel.

Keen to understand the younger generation, the Establishment sent out first for a butterfly and then for a wheel.

They spent the rest of the day trying to stick the one to the other, but with no success.

Sit-ins

The Sixties witnessed an increasing amount of student rest, often involving lengthy sit-ins. Young people would sit down, often on top of one another. It was all part of what was termed the Generation Lap.

'With-it' young people with long hair demonstrated against the so-called Grosvenor Square, or President Johnson ('LBW') as he was known. Other notable demonstrations of the time included Cookery, Yoga, Origami and Dental Meditation.

Demonstrations were more idealistic in America, and more glamorous in France, but at least in Britain they were much less crowded. Whereas the American protest movement took as its slogan 'Tune in, Turn On and Drop Out', the British protest movement preferred the more relaxing, 'Tune In, Turn Over and Drop Off'.

In America, the Civil Rights movement came to a head with a speech from Dr Martin Luther King. But times had moved on. In this, his only British interview, Dr King came up against a new, less deferential type of BBC interviewer:

INTERVIEWER: So, Dr King, as I understand it you claim to have had some sort of a dream.

DR KING: I have a dream that one day this nation will—

INTERVIEWER: Let me stop you there, Dr King. A lot of our listeners will be thinking to themselves, why should we be worrying about the nocturnal habits of, if you'll forgive me, this unelected man few if any of us have ever heard of?

DR KING: I have a dream that one day this nation will rise up and live out the true meaning of its creed: 'We hold these truths to be self-evident; that all men are created equal.' I have a dream that—

INTERVIEWER: But the big question is, when exactly? That's what our listeners will be wanting to know. They'll be saying, 'It's all very well saying you've had a dream, we've all had dreams, every night we have dreams, but if you believe that this dream of yours is going to come true, then what precisely is the timescale we're talking about?

DR KING: I have a dream that one day on the red hills of Georgia, the sons of former slaves—

INTERVIEWER: But they're not exactly red, now, are they? I'm not sure you're being totally straightforward with us, Dr King. After all, the latest research suggests that the hills you call – and I quote – 'red', are not in fact red at all. What do you have to say to that, Dr King?

DR KING: – the sons of former slaves and the sons of former slave-owners will be able to sit down together at the table of brotherhood. I have a dream that one day—

INTERVIEWER: I'm sorry, Dr King, but you've already said that. But where exactly is this so-called 'table of brotherhood', Dr King? By all accounts, no one seems to have seen it yet. And some sources are suggesting it doesn't even exist. Well, does it, Dr King? Yes or no, Dr King?

DR KING: I have a dream that my four little children will one day live—

INTERVIEWER: Yes or no?

DR KING: – in a nation where they will not be judged by the colour of their—

INTERVIEWER: I'm going to have to rush you, Dr King.

DR KING: – will not be judged by the colour of their skin but by the content of their—

INTERVIEWER: I'm sorry, We're going to have to leave it there. And now over to Steve with the sport.

Flour Power

'If you're going to San Francisco,' sang Scott McDougall in 1967, 'Be sure to wear some flour in your hair.'

Flour Power was based on the idea of transcendental self-raising, often without much dough. Among the Flour Power gurus were the famous Indian yoghurt, Margarhini, whose supporters claimed they couldn't tell him from butter.

Flour Power gave birth to the Hippie Movement. This involved very little movement, though a hippie might occasionally nod his head to signal approval.

The hippies were best known for the Summer of Lav. Thousands of young people gathered in fields with only three mobile toilets between them, one of them temporarily out of order.

The hippies soon made way for other, hairier, movements. These included:

- **Yippies:** founded by Tom and Jerry.
- **Dippies:** branch of the RAC Liberation Front, sworn to dip their headlights when approaching an oncoming vehicle.
- **Lippies:** unlike the Hippies, always answered back.
- **Nippies:** queue-bargers at Woodstock.
- **Pippies:** fruitarians.
- **Tippies:** at rock festivals, always left ten per cent on the stage for the bass player.

CHAPTER 44

The Condition of Ulcer

In the late 1960s, the British discovered Northern Ireland, later diagnosed as Ulcer.

Northern Ireland was famous for the Troubles, a centuries-old dispute understood only by a handful of historians, who all disagreed about it anyway.

On the one side were the Onionists, who were not to be sniffed at. They were led by the Reverend Elvis Presley, who campaigned under the slogan 'Nose Surrender'. The Onionists wore suits and bowler hats and spent their time calling for apologies.

On the other side were the Publicans, led by Gerry Addams of the famous Addams Family, who campaigned under the slogan 'Bits Out'. The Publicans wore balaclavas and spent their time refusing to apologise.

CHAPTER 45

The First Man on the Moon

In July 1969 the American astronaut Neil Armstrong became the first man on the moon. Happily, no Britons were involved. 'One small step for man,' he was overheard admitting. He landed at 3.56 in the morning, when he knew that ordinary decent Britons would be asleep.

Unlike the British, the Americans had never won the World Cup, had their own Royal Family or climbed Everest. So they had spent a fortune trying to put the first man on the moon, using the latest science and technology to give them an unfair advantage.

The American astronauts even had special suits made for the expedition, and travelled there not with grappling-irons, ropes and hard-wearing boots but just sitting down in a rocket.

In the same month, top golfer Tony Jacklin became the

first Briton to win the British Open, wearing just a thin V-neck jersey and a pair of lightweight slacks, and using only clubs and a ball.

The British Space Project had no need for special suits or the very latest technology. Instead, it involved the imaginative use of elastic bands, balsawood and a dab of glue. In the end, we decided it wasn't worth the bother. Deciding not to bother was what the British did best.

CHAPTER 46

The Royal Family in the Sixties

In the Sixties, the Royal Family began to worry that they were going out of fashion, so Prince Phlip said they should all wear kilts and hold weekly barbecues on television.

At that time, the Royal Family still had very few members. This was before its big recruitment drive of the 1970s and 1980s. But once the general public had seen them enjoying barbecues on television, everyone wanted to join. So by the 1990s the Royal Family had far more members than it could cope with, and some were forced to stand.

The decade ended with the Investment of the Prince of Wails in a Carnival Castle. The Prince had learnt to speak Welsh specially, or sppyyllcllyly. But on the same day, the Rolling Stones played a concert in Hyde Park, so only two people turned up to the Investment: Lord Jones of Snowdon, who came dressed as a pageboy, and Queen Elizabeth 11th, who came as herself.

The 1960s

1. The World Cup
   (i) If the USA had managed to win the World Cup in 1966, would they have still felt the need to prove themselves by sending a man to the moon?
   (ii) Explain, within reason, how the first man on the moon failed to stop the inexorable rise of Adolf Hitler.

2. Who was the Legless Man? *Answer on one side of the photograph only.*
   (a) Douglas Bader
   (b) Douglas Bareshanks Jr
   (c) Lord Privy Seal
   (d) The Garter King at Arms
   (e) The Chief Whip
   (f) The Lord Chambermaid
   (g) Selwyn Lewd
   (h) Above of the nun

3. Who was the legless ma'am? *Answer in a straight line, one step at a time.*
   (a) Princess Margaret
   (b) Queen Elizabeth the Queen Mother
   (c) The Duchess of Windsor
   (d) None of the above

4. Is this the Northern Ireland question: If not, what is?

5. What would have happened to Mick Jigger if he had been able to get satisfaction? Answer on both sides of the sheets.

6. 'This is the darning of the Age of Aquarius.' Why did it need mending?

7. Where is the Global Village?

8. Source A:
'Barbara tells me Jim heard from George that Dick told Roy that Harold no longer trusts Denis because he repeated what Barbara told Jim. This is all very interesting. I tell Barbara that Jim told Denis that Harold thinks Roy told Dick what George heard from me. In the evening, I speak to the TGWU, urging them to keep personalities out of it and stick to the issues.'

> entry for 10 May 1968, *Diaries of Tony Benn*, page 28,931.

Read Source A before answering the following questions.
- (a) What did Roy tell Dick?
- (b) Why does Harold no longer trust Denis?
- (c) What did George hear from Roy?

9. Who lived Chez Guevara?

10. Answer any 4 of the following 3 questions:

- (i) Who's afraid of Virginia Woolf?
- (ii) Voulez-vous coucher avec moi?
- (iii) He would, wouldn't he?

11. Source B:

'Ten years later, when I was the most famous radio personality in the country, I went back to Millfield. As a showbiz celebrity I had the accessories to match – an E-Type Jag and a gorgeous bunny girl in the shortest mini-skirt ever invented'

from *Living Legend: The Autobiography of Tony Blackburn*

Read Source B, then answer the following questions.

(i) (a) Employing diagrams where necessary, describe the meaning and purpose of a 'mini-skirt'.

(b) In what way can the mini-skirt be said to have been 'invented'?

(ii) In this passage, Blackburn confesses to having a 'radio personality'. How would one diagnose this disorder? What were its symptoms? How was it treated?

(iii) An 'E-Type Jag' was:

(a) A syringe

(b) A pill

(c) A musical instrument

(d) A vehicle.

(iv) A 'bunny girl' was:

(a) A young female rabbit

(b) A woman who dressed up as a rabbit

(c) A rabbit who dressed up as a woman

(d) An amusing girl suffering from a cold.

(v) Vocabulary. Render the following Blackburnian words and phrases into modern English, using only one side of the paper:

(a) Byood ivul (b) Thereyego (c) Van tastig (d) Udderly urmay zing

(vi) (i) Who or what was a 'disc-jockey'?
    (ii) Why?

12. Do you know the way to San Jose?

THE SEVENTIES

As the clock strikes midnight on New Year's Eve, 1969, the smiles are wiped off the faces of all ordinary decent Britons. For the Conservatives, Edward Teeth brings in the three day week, for the Liberals, Jeremy Throat fails to murder Scott of the Antarctic, and for Labour, Harold Wilson rewards Lord Crippen and Sir Norman Bates in his resignation honours list.

The vulgarity of the decades reaches new heights in the arts, when The Six Pastilles swear at Bill Grumpy, and Diana Cooper takes 'School's Out' to the top of the charts.

CHAPTER 47

Depressing Result

Many foreign newspapers put about rumours that West Germany had beaten England in the first round of the 1970 World Cup. But of course it didn't count, because:

(a) we weren't playing on our home ground and
(b) we had only just won the real World Cup, so we obviously needed time to get our breath back.

English soccer experts agree there have been no proper World Cups since then, and there won't be any in future, or at least not until England wins.

Depressing Conversion

In 1971, just after the Beatles split up, the pound was decimated, which made everyone even more depressed. Decimation meant that the Penny Farthing was abolished, causing Britain to ride around on a cycle of depression.

As Britain took to the Continental way of adding up, what had once been clear now became muddled.

Where there had once been a handy 144 pennies in a pound, there were now just 100 kilometres, and where there were an easy-to-remember twelve pennies in a shilling there were now five kilowatts, and that was no help because ounces didn't exist any more. A half-crown had been two and six (or 2/6), and now you couldn't get change for an ordinary Fahrenheit.

To work out what on earth was going on, everybody was forced to keep this handy table in their pockets:

OLD	NEW
12 pennies	100 degrees centigrade
100 degrees Fahrenheit	50 new pee
1 packet of sugar	25 metres
tuppence ha'penny	1 kilowatt

A Depressing Week

Ordinary, decent Britons were further muddled and depressed when Mr Edward Teeth, the Unmemorable Leader of the Conservatory Party, converted the country to the Continental system of the Three Day Week.

From now on, he announced, the week would consist of just three days – Tuesday, Wednesday and Thursday, to run simultaneously. At the same time, he proposed a mix-up of the historic old counties of Britain, so that Shropshire would now be known as Surrey, Surrey as Yorkshire, Yorkshire as Devon, and so on. He promised it would make things a lot simpler.

To further complicate matters, in 1974 Mr Teeth decided that instead of one General Election every five years, there would be two General Elections every one year. But, by mistake, in 1974 he lost the second election. He spent the rest of his life trying to find it, but without any success.

Your Guide to the Key Marginals in the October 1974 General Election

Barking

Blair, Linda

Bokassa, Emperor

Fairbairn, N.

Paisley, Rev. I.

Powell, Rt Hon. J. E.

Pyke, Magnus

Von Daniken, E.

Bath

Osbourne, O.

Rotten, J.

Berks

McLaren, M.

Moon, K.

Phillips, Capt. M.

Wyatt, W.

Bickering

Bessell, P.

Newton, A. 'G'.

Napley Sir D.

Rinka.

Scott, N.

Thorpe, Rt Hon. J.

Blandford

Aspel, M.

Chalmers, J.

Crowther, L.

Doonican, V.

Whittaker, R.

Boreham

Connors, J.

Fowler, Rt Hon. Norman

Henderson, Sir N.

Rainier, Prince
Straw, J.

Bray
Bristol, Marquess of
Fermoy, Lady R.
Maitland, Lady O.
Rothermere, Lady B.

The Broads
Dors, D.
Kent, Princess M. of
Khashoggi, S.
McKinney, J.
Windsor, B

Bucks
Hunt, G.
Lichfield, Earl of
Llewellyn, R.
McEnroe, J.
Mower, P.

Burley
Amin, Gen. I.
Manning, B.
Presley, E.
Smith, C.
Weidenfeld, G.

Bushey

CHAPTER 48

The 1970s was a time of scandals, but Britain's scandals were always bigger and better than America's. In the 1960s, we had led the way, and we had no intention of letting them catch up.

Waterbottle: A Minor American Scandal of No Importance

In America, Waterbottle was already very hot. President Richard M. Nixon had secretly sent his plumbers over the road to fix a faulty waterbottle in a bedroom occupied by his rival, George McGovern, whom he suspected of having a made-up name to give him a better chance of winning.

This prompted two Hollywood journalists – Robert Redford and Dustin Hoffman – to think that everything might not be quite as it should be. By running back and forth through their newspaper offices at great speed, they discovered that President Nixon's middle name was Milhous, and that his plumbers (Bob the Handyman, Spiral Anew) had been overcharging.

Under pressure, Nixon threatened to appear before Congress in peach. This prompted a public outcry, and he resigned. His successor was Gerald Ford, an Unmemorable President. On being told he was now President, Ford coughed politely and continued with his round of golf.

Four British Scandals that Depressed the World

1. *The Throat Scandal*

   Jeremy Throat was the Leader of the Liberal Party, which consisted mainly of himself. Some thought him a little peculiar because:

   (a) he wore a double-breasted waistcoat and went round leaping over gates in a hovercraft;
   (b) he hired former pilots to shoot Great Danes accidentally on purpose.

   Eventually, he was arrested and charged with being the Leader of the Liberal Party, a charge he strenuously denied. He claimed that at the time in question he had been far too busy plotting the deaths of former male models. The jury could find no evidence of a Liberal Party, so he was propositioned on all counts.

   His former friend, Scott of the Antarctic, went back to pursuing his former career, modelling woolly jumpers in nippy conditions while being pulled along by Huskies. He said he might be some time, but never came back.

2. *The Honours Scandal*

Historians now believe that Prime Minister Harold Wilson probably retired in 1977, or somewhere around then.

He left strict instructions on luxury lavender toilet tissue that the following persons should receive honours:

The Gay Brothers. Knighthoods for Sir Ronald, Sir Reginald and Sir Charles Gay, for services to the protection industry.

Lord Crippen, for services to medicine.

Dame Linda Lovelace, for services to the motion industry.

Sir Norman Bates, for services to the hotel and leisure industries.

The list caused a major scandal. The Conservatives were furious that he had overlooked former Conservative Home Secretary Reginald Muddling, though at least there was a knighthood for their fleet-footed Chairman, Sir Edward du Can-Can.

3. *The Fourth Man Scandal*

Sir Anthony Blunt turned out to have been anything but. On closer investigation it emerged that, instead of painting the Queen's portrait, for years he had secretly been the Fourth Beatle.

Having struck up a youthful friendship with the First, Second and Third Beatles, Blunt had secretly released hundreds of records. When his home was raided by the secret service (or M25) they uncovered a Beatle wig, a pair of flared trousers and the charred remains of a used drum kit.

4. *The Corruption Scandal*

Businessmen in the Seventies were all arrested on charges of bribery, corruption and excessive sideburns and put in prison. They were then let out and encouraged to rejoin the House of Lords, where they could lend their wealth of experience to the topics of the day. A former Home Secretary, Reginald Muddling, was also involved, but he was let off on the grounds that he couldn't be expected to make head or tail of it all.

CHAPTER 49

Depressing Shocks

As the Seventies continued, more and more performers set out to shock. It was the error of Glitter Rock. From America, Diana Cooper, covered with mascara, sang the provocative anti-Establishment anthem 'School's Out' while biting the head off a free-range chicken.

Last Mango in Paris was set amid a fruit-and-veg shortage in the French capital. It featured a man and woman who meet regularly, but never get on first-name terms. *The Brevilles*, by British director Ken Wrestle, showed what happens when a toasted sandwich-maker goes wrong.

Germaine Greer published her women's book, *The Female Lunch*. It was hailed as a feminist breakthrough by the critical Establishment. They all said they were frankly amazed that so many long words had come out of that pretty little head of hers.

Pun Rock

The birth of Pun Rock can be dated to 1976, when the controversial young group the Six Pastilles appeared on television swerving at the veteran interviewer Bill Grumpy.

On stage, the Six Pastilles sat in the direction of the

audience. Their songs were full of dad language. The Six Pastilles released a single called 'God Shave the Clean'.

Other notable Pun Rock groups included The Darned, The Class and Generating Eggs.

CHAPTER 50

Depressing Disappearances

It was a decade of power cuts and black-outs. When the lights came back on again, a number of people had vanished. They included:

Carlos the Jackal
Carlos the Jackal – real name Charles Jackal – was largely responsible for everything that went wrong in the Seventies, including the Three Day Week, Waterbottle, Tootal Co-ordinates and Bucks Fizz, the Eurovision Spooner Contest winners.

He first came to prominence when President de Gaulle, with typical French *de haut en bas*, refused to acknowledge he had just been assassinated by him. He was played in the film by English actor Edward the Fox.

Throughout his career, Carlos the Jackal kept escaping from the police by growing a moustache and then – the minute they had run past – shaving it off again. He had over twenty different passports, each with a different photograph in which – in a dramatic double-bluff – he looked exactly the same.

It is not now known whether he is alive or dead, or somewhere in between. Some say he can be spotted every weekday presenting the weather on BBC3, but no one has yet gone to the bother of finding out.

Lord Lucan

Like many aristocrats before him, Lord Lucan mistook his nanny for his wife.

In a terrible muddle, he killed his nanny, which was still illegal in those days. Next he disappeared into thin air, never to be seen again. But over the years, there have been many sightings. These include:

- leading the pop group Queen in a white vest and armband at Wembley
- posing as Carlos the Jackal in a passport booth
- skulking underwater in Loch Ness
- lurking beneath a white beard and red cape in a specially constructed grotto in Debenhams, Ipswich.

During a power-cut, the Postmaster General disappeared. He was later found to be living in Australia. He had made the elementary mistake of pretending to be Lord Lucan, and was arrested by police who thought he was Freddie Mercury.

Leaving his swimming trunks on a beach, Stonehouse returned to England, where he was arrested for indecent exposure. He stood trial on a charge of pretending to be himself. He pleaded not guilty, but no one believed him and he was sent to prison.

CHAPTER 51

Depressing Glimmer of Light

The only glimmer of light in the Seventies was provided by the marriage of the Queen's daughter, HRH Princess Anne, to Captain Phillips, a horse.

'This is a fairytale wedding,' observed the Archbishop of Canterbury, 'between a horse and his rider.'

The crowds went wild as Princess Anne rode her intended into Westminster Abbey.

On the strength of this unusual pairing, Princess Anne was awarded the title of BBC Sports Personality of the Year; Captain Phillips gained three rosettes.

CHAPTER 52

Depressing Fashion

In the 1970s, everyone wore platform shoes, including HM the Queen. This created a problem when she posed for her portrait on stamps and coins. Stamps dating from this decade show only the bottom half of her face.

Depressing Cuisine

Nouve Hell Cuisine was a completely new type of cuisine, specially developed for those who wanted to eat expensively, but weren't hungry. It consisted of a slice of kiwi fruit in the middle of a very large plate, overlaid with a crop-circle pattern in maroon.

Depressing Tyrants

Emperor Bicasso
Emperor Bicasso was an obsessive cubist, cutting up his enemies into small pieces then rearranging them.

The Ayatollah Khomily
The Ayatollah gained his nickname after saying, 'Ayatollah you so,' at the downfall of his enemy, the Shah of Rain. He

spent many years in Paris winning over his people by wearing a long beard and sitting in the corner, scowling.

General Amin

General Idi Amin began life as a joke in *Punch* magazine, but, like so many jokes, it got out of control.

Depressing Arts

Among the bestselling books of the decade were *Small Is Pitiful*, *The Joy of Socks* and *Glove Story*.

Watership Down was a book about a colony of accountants written by a former rabbit. The cookery book bestsellers were headed by Erica Thong's *The Fear of Frying*. Alex Haley's *Hoots!* traced the author's ancestry to an ancient troupe of Scots impersonators.

The great movie success of the decade was *Jaws*, about a seaside community threatened by sharks. This was followed by many copy-cat films, including *Clause*, a rural community threatened by a contract lawyer, and *Baws*, a retirement community threatened by raconteurs.

CHAPTER 53

The Winter of Discontent

To ensure he presented his sunniest face to the British electorate, Prime Minister James Calorgas decided to relocate to a beach villa in Bermuda.

There he spent his days sipping piña coladas in a straw hat, engaging in bridge-building exercises with world statesmen such as Discard G'uesthouse of France, Helmet Shift of West Germany and President Jimmy Crater of America. In the afternoons, President Crater liked to go out jogging in a headband and collapse in a heap. In the evenings, they would all enjoy a sizzling cheese fondue, the eating craze that was sweeping the world. But Mr Calorgas was not used to foreign food, hence his nickname, 'Runny Jim'.

News never reached Mr Calorgas of the Winter of Discontent, when everyone in Britain went on strike. It was what the British did best.

Great piles of Seventies rubbish were left in the streets, including the works of Eric von Daniken, *The Complete Poldark*, a Rubik's Cube, a Breville Toasted-sandwich Maker, *Leo Sayer's Greatest Hits*, a case of Blue Nun, two Black Forest gâteaux, a catering pack of Ski yoghurt and a selection of tank tops.

Arriving at Heathrow Airport in a garland of flowers and a straw skirt, Prime Minister Calorgas wiggled his hips, brought out a pair of castanets and sang, 'Crisis? What crisis?' to a calypso beat.

Sadly, he had misjudged the rhythm of the electorate and lost the subsequent General Election.

CHAPTER 54

Depressing Christmas Broadcast

As the Seventies wore on, the media grew ever more intrusive. The Royal Family, which for so long had been treated with reverence, were now subjected regularly to intrusive cross-questioning, as this extract from HM the Queen's Christmas Broadcast makes all too clear:

HM THE QUEEN: Traditionally, Christmas is a time at which people the world over agree to put aside their differences and join together in one purpose. Over the past year, I have visited a great many countries and—

HUMPHRYS: Let me just stop you there, if I may. What exactly do you *mean* when you say 'people the world over'?

HM THE QUEEN: Well, um, I suppose what I mean is, um, people all over the world.

HUMPHRYS: Correct me if I'm wrong, but as I see it you're trying to claim that *people all over the world* traditionally join together *in one purpose* at Christmas. With all due respect, Your Majesty, I think a lot of our listeners are going to be saying to themselves, 'This lady may go around calling herself the Queen but, frankly, she's living in Cloud Cuckoo Land!'

HM THE QUEEN: Well, I'm sorry if they, er – look, I have got rather a lot more of my speech to get through.

HUMPHRYS: And, furthermore, they'll be asking themselves *why on earth* they have to listen to this hogwash when they could be putting their feet up on Christmas afternoon. So what do you say to that, Your Majesty?

HM THE QUEEN: Well, I was only trying to be nice. And I do have rather more of this to read out—

HUMPHRYS: I'm afraid that's all we've got time for. Now it's over to Steve with the sports news.

CHAPTER 55

Three British Triumphs to Lift the Depression

(1) *A British Champion*

In 1977, the Women's Final at Wimbledon was won by a British woman, Virginia Wade, in gumboots. It was the year

126

of the Queen's Jubilee, so Britain was allowed to retain the title for at least another twenty-five years.

(2) *A British King*

The same year saw the death of Elvis Parsley, causing the title 'The King of Rock 'n' Roll' to pass directly to Cliff Richard of Great Britain, who has held it ever since.

A month later, the Italian singer Maria Callas died. Once again, it was a British singer, Cilla Black, who stepped into her shoes.

(3) *A British Aeroplane*

The supersonic airliner Concorde was the product of a twin argument between Britain and France. The governments of both countries saw it as the only way of getting Sir David Frostbite across the Atlantic in time for his first television programme of the week, and back again in time for the next.

Concorde's first scheduled passenger service took off on 21 January 1976. There was room inside for only eight passengers, four on each side of the aisle. They were:

Sir David Frostbite	Janie Jones
Bernie Cornfeld	Lord Lucan
Rt Hon John Stonehouse	Andrew 'Gino' Newton
Rinka	Lord Kagan

In accordance with the mood of the time, it was planned to spray Concorde with glitter and give it a tank top. But the growing depression caused the designers to cut back on these extras, and instead to give Concorde her trademark hang-dog expression.

A British Pop Sensation

Agnetha, Benny, Björn and Anni-Frid – four very British singers who together formed the British world-beating pop group otherwise known as ABBA.

Abba – who all hailed from Swindon – first came to prominence when they won the Eurovision Song Contest for Britain back in 1974, with that very British hit 'Waterloo', which celebrated another other great British victory by our troops at Trafalgar.

CHAPTER 56

The Dawn of a New Error

When Mr Edward Teeth was forcibly ejected as leader of the Conservatories, he was replaced by Mrs Thatcherism, a Memorable Prime Minister. Mrs Thatcherism was twinned with Monetarism, the invention of Milton Keynes, the new town divided against itself.

Margaret Thatcherism spent her childhood in a grocer's shop. Her father gave her a slicing machine to operate and she immediately set to work dividing opinion.

When Mr Teeth made her Education Secretary, she went around playgrounds siphoning off the children's milk into a container lorry.

Campaigning against Mr Teeth for the leadership of the Conservatories, she put on a funny face and grinned a lot, saying, 'The Lady's not for Gurning.' This endeared her to the party frightful, who thought it high time they were led by someone they were terrified of.

Following the Summer of Discotheque and the Winter of Discontent, the decade ended with Margaret Thatcherism standing outside No. 10 Downing Street, reciting the memorable words, 'Where there is disco, may we bring harmony.'

The 1970s

Write your name on top of each sheet. Write it over and over again, with more and more elaborate curlicues beneath it. Now draw smiley faces inside each B, D, G, O, P and Q.

Wait until the little hand is on 12 and the big hand is on 11 before getting round to these questions.

Time up.

1 (i) Why do its detractors refer to it as a Common Market? Explode, with diagrams.

  (ii) Would you rather be:

     (a) In Europe but not of Europe?
     (b) On Europe but not inside Europe?
     (c) Over Europe but not above Europe?
     (d) Out of Europe but not behind Europe?

 (iii) Did anyone say it would be EC?

2. 'The unacceptable face of catapultism'. Edward Teeth, 15th May 1973.

    What made Ron Lho forfeit his catapult?

3. To what extent did Glam Rock prevent the rise of Adolf Hitler?

4. Who, if anyone, was the Prime Minister between Harold Wilson and Mrs Thatcherism? Did he wear glasses? List what you cannot remember about him, giving examples.

5. Two little boys have two little toys. Each has a wooden horse. How many wooden horses do they have, to the nearest ten?

6. If the Bhagwam Sree Rajneesh was the leader of the Orange people, who was the leader of the Republicans?

7. Draw a scale-map of Barbara Castle, with ramparts.

8. Decimalisation: If a half-crown was two and six, then what was two and six?

9. Why was the Minor Strike taken so seriously?

10. Here is a list of five events from the 1970s, and five effects that were the result of these events. Match up the event with the effect.

EVENTS
  (i) The Winter of Discontent.
 (ii) A lava lamp, a safari suit, a blackcurrant cheesecake and the Nolan Sisters are added together.
(iii) Hot Pants.

EFFECTS
 (a) David Frostbite.
 (b) A vulgar fraction.
 (c) Clarence, the Cross-eyed Lion.

Answers: ia; iib; iiic.

11. Do you (a) Agree or (b) disagree with this statement? Give reasons.

12. Study Source A.

Source A:
(a) What does Source A tell us about the state of the world in 1979?
(b) 'The cartoonist suggests that this was a time of optimism and cheer.' Do you agree with this statement? How does the cartoonist hint at an opposite interpretation?

13.
(a) Is there life on Mars?
(b) Should I stay or should I go?
(c) Is this the way to Amarillo?

THE EIGHTIES

An Avaricious Decade

The decade is characterised by greed and avarice. By the end of the 1980s, shopping has been officially accepted as an Olympic sport.

In the City, brash young floor-traders smoke pinstripe cigars and wear red braces on their teeth. They chain-smoke their Filofaxes as they trade away the floors they stand up on.

But inevitably the balloon goes up, and this leads to a Big Bang.

CHAPTER 57

Michael's Foot

'Runny Jim' Calorgas had resigned the leadership of the Labour Party in celebration at losing the 1979 General Election. He was led away beaming, repeating, 'Christmas? What Christmas?' to himself over and over again.

The Party now had to choose their next loser from (a) Denis Healey, a pair of veteran eyebrows, or (b) Michael's Foot.

They plumped for Michael's Foot, which was on the left.

The Rise and Fall of the SDP

In protest, a new party, the SDP, was formed in 1981 by a group calling themselves the Fang of Gore. They were four individuals bound together by mutual distrust.

As the Eighties began, the group issued a statement called 'The Greenhouse Effect', which they described as a stone-throwing exercise. They aimed to break bridges and build the mould.

The four consisted of:

Lord Roy Junket

In a memorable political career, Lord Junket had held every position known to man, plus several known only to God (who, he later revealed, was a distant relative, and the possessor of a perfectly reasonable second-rate mind).

Mrs Whirly Shillinghams

Mrs Shillinghams threw on the nearest tablecloth and rushed around the country seeing both sides of the question. She appealed to the part of the electorate that wanted much more time to get ready. A keen theoretician, her best-selling books included *Politics Is For People*, its follow-up *Maybe Not Exclusively* and, the final work in the trilogy, *But On the Other Hand*.

Dr David Own

A former Foreign Secateur, Dr Own was a force to be reckoned with. Good at dividing, but bad at ruling, he set his sights on an Own Goal, and achieved it.

The fourth member of the SDP was Unmemorable.

Sadly, the leaders of the SDP didn't see eye-to-eye on the need for consensus. Dr Own led a breakaway group, so they changed their name to the DP; then Lord Roy Junket left to join the Liberals, and they changed their name once again, this time to the P.

Finally, in an attempt to retain their distinctive identity, they changed their name to the ' ', which they have remained ever since.

CHAPTER 58

Poor Stanley

Buoyed up by his late wife's success in the hit musical *Evita*, General Belgrano of Argentina sent his men to invade the Falkland Islands in 1982.

The Falklands were inhabited by an ordinary decent Briton, Poor Stanley. The Argentinians held Poor Stanley hostage in the village hall for the duration of hostilities, giving him nothing to eat but goose (green).

On hearing the news of Poor Stanley's capture, the Foreign Secretary, Lord Carry-on, resigned. His deputy Francis Prim took over. Prim was calm, John nott.

Mrs Thatcherism vowed to win back the Falklands, and so sent the entire British armed forces eight thousand miles across the Atlantic in their boat.

Poor Stanley was eventually liberated by the lanky English journalist Max Height. On hearing the good news, Mrs Thatcherism memorably said, 'We have become a grandmother.'

Five More Memorable Sayings of Mrs Thatcherism

1. Advisers advise and ministers are told.
2. There is no such thing as sobriety.
3. I fight on, and I fight the wind.
4. Fritters!
5. Lechery with a smile on its face (of Cecil Parkinson).

CHAPTER 59

British Inventors Rue the World

The Sinclair C5 was an entirely new type of vehicle, part scooter, part wheelie-bin. It was called after its British inventor Sir C5, who brilliantly designed it to indicate external weather conditions to the driver by automatically toppling over in high winds.

Only a few people ever bought one, which made it even more exclusive. By the end, the C5 was so exclusive that they stopped making it.

Another great British world-beater of the time was the DiLegal motorcar, exclusively manufactured in Belfast by John DiLegal. It was cleverly designed so that when you opened the door, the roof came off, and when you opened the roof, the engine exploded. Building exploding cars was what the British did best.

The Hittler Diaries

In 1983, the *Sundry Times* was excited to discover sixty volumes called 'The Diaries of Adolf Hittler' under a printing press.

Allowing time for the ink to dry, they gave them to the extinguished historian Professor Hugh Very-Ropey, who immediately pronounced them orthodontic.

Sundry Times readers were fascinated to read the following revelations from the pen of Adolf Hittler:

DAY ONE: Dear Diary, Today I decided to start a diary! I hope no one says it's not authentic, 'cos they'd be wrong!

DAY TWO: Day two of my diary!

DAY THREE: Diary going well! It's still completely authentic!

DAY FOUR: Four days of keeping my authentic diary! That's nearly a week!

DAY FIVE: Diary coming on apace! Each day seems even more authentic than the last!

DAY SIX: By tomorrow, I will have been keeping an authentic diary for a week! It could be worth a fortune in, say, forty or fifty years' time!

DAY SEVEN: Dear Diary, I have been keeping you authentically for a week! Well done me! Signed Adolf Hittler.

Sadly, the Hittler Diaries were revealed to be a forgery. Handwriting experts pointed out that the Führer had never been known to draw a smiley face in the *o* of each Adolf.

Knock-Knock

After Michael's Foot lost the 1983 General Election, the Labour Party elected Neil Knock-Knock, an after-dinner joke.

Knock-Knock decided to take on the so-called Lard Heft in his party by repeating himself over and over again until they could bear it no more. His opponents in the Dilettante Tendency believed in Claws 4, whereby the workers owned reproductions.

He set his ideas out 'briefly, briskly, concisely and, furthermore, succinctly, crisply and, wherever possible, sharply' in a three-and-a-half-hour speech. It began:

I hope not only to talk but to converse, and not only to converse but to prattle, and not only to prattle but to verbalise; and in so doing, I fully, thoroughly and wholly intend to discuss, negotiate, inform and communicate; and, moreover, and I say this to you now, I have no wish to be long-winded, loquacious, verbose or in any way mouthy, prolix, voluble or effusive . . .

At one point, it looked as though Mr Knock-Knock was about to be voted Prime Minister. But he kept falling over into the sea and shouting, 'och aye the noo' at rallies in Sheffield, so the electorate decided against.

CHAPTER 60

The Thatcherism Years

Mrs Thatcherism is remembered for two things:

  (a) The way she came in
  (b) The way she went out.

Eleven years separated these two events. They were known as the Thatcherism Years. They were full of memorable Affairs, now largely forgotten.

Two Affairs Best Forgotten

The Westlife Affair

Michael Vaseline (nickname: Marzipan) was a Tory high-flier with big hair. He wanted a helicopter to help him fly his hair all over the country.

Vaseline was determined that Westlife should build him his helicopter, but Mrs Thatcherism preferred the rival claims of the S Club Seven consortium.

One day, Michael Vaseline could take it no longer and stormed into a cabinet. He then embarked on a lengthy campaign to become Prime Minister by going up and down the country denying he wanted to be Prime Minister.

The Pole Tax Affair

Towards the end of her reign, Mrs Thatcherism decided to tax everyone who kept a pole in their home in case they should decide to use it to mount a neighbourhood attack, or Community Charge.

She never used the term Pole Tax herself, preferring to describe it as the Pool Tax, targeted at the better-off, or the Peel Tax, targeted at litter louts.

The Polo Tax was found, on closer examination, to have a hole in its centre.

CHAPTER 61

A Decade of British Triumphs

In the 1980s, Britain regained her sense of ambition. From now on, she would no longer be the poor man of Europe: she would be the poor man of the World.

It was a decade of British triumphs. In 1982, top British film-makers David Putty and Colin Welloff won an Oscar with *Chariots for Hire*, in which top British athletes Liddell and Large raced each other round an Oxford college on quad bikes.

Clutching his Oscar, Colin Welloff memorably said, 'The British are coming!' Sure enough, seventeen years later yet another British film was short-listed for an Academy Award.

In the same year, top overweight cricketer Ian Bottom single-handedly led the England cricket team to win the Asses. Such a triumph meant it would be unsporting to win the Asses again for another twenty years so we didn't bother.

In 1984, top British cake-icers Orville and Bean won first prize at the World Iced Caking Championships for their version of Ravel's 'Blancmange'.

Pop music in the Eighties was dominated by groups such as Droan Droan, Spandau Ballsup, Adam Aunt and Depressive Mode. They all danced with great difficulty and thus became known as the New Rheumatics.

Back Holes

The bestselling book of the decade was *The Time History of Briefs* by Stephen Hawking. It sought to explain many baffling mysteries associated with the history of briefs such as Back Holes and the Big Bulge, and presented a unifying theory of the Y-front.

Do briefs run backwards? How short is a boxer? Is the elastic infinite? Can you glimpse a guiding hand behind your briefs?

The book offered an explanation for the whole of creation. But, sadly, no one ever got to the end so it remains a mystery.★

Stephen Hawking became as famous as his book. 'Did you see Stephen Hawking?' eagle-eyed tourists would ask one another in the streets of Cambridge. 'He was just clearing his throat,' would come the reply.

Cowshed Revisited

The television triumph of the decade was undoubtedly *Cowshed Revisited*, from the novel by veteran double-kisser Evelyn Mwaugh.

Margaret Dribble writes:

Cowshed Revisited tells the tale of a haggard young Oxford undergraduate called Ryder who takes his unhappily married teddy bear, Sebastian, to stay in a stately home. Over a sumptuous four-course dinner, with fine wine and a full array of family silver, they are converted to Catholicism.

★ Most popular page to put down *The Time History of Briefs* for a bit of a breather, never to pick it up again: 1, 3, 15, 21, 31, 33.

CHAPTER 62

The Question Mark Invasion

In the 1980s?
    The pause and?
    The question mark?
    Began to appear in random?
    Places when the young?
    Were talking?
    This was put down?
    To the growing influence?
    Of Australian soap operas?
    Such as *Neighbours*?

Liver Aid

Liver Aid was the first concert in which pop stars told ordinary decent Britons how to behave. It was thus a Memorable Watershed (see *Watersheds, Memorable*). Until then, pop stars had behaved badly, and ordinary decent Britons had disapproved; from then on, the positions were reversed.

Twenty-five years later, heads of state continue to line up on an annual basis with their heads bowed and their hands held out. They are then rapped over the knuckles and told they must try harder by top Irish sunglasses Bonio and Sir Barb Gedoff.

Puppies

The Eighties became famous for grouping people together in Acronyms (Archly Capitalised Rather Odd Names for Young Members of Society). Many of them – Yuppies, Preppies, Nimbys – did not last long. One that endures is Puppies (young offspring of dogs).

CHAPTER 63

Three Royal Mishaps

Throughout the 1980s, the Royal Family both multiplied and divided, with exciting new members added every few months, some of them subtracting from the mystique.

The Prince and Princess of Wails

The wedding of the Prince and Princess of Wails took place in 1981. Looking back, keen observers felt that, even at this early stage, everything was not as it should be.

'Do you take this woman to be your lawfully wedded wife?' asked the Archbishop of Canterbury.

'Whatever that means,' replied the Prince of Wails, with a shrug. No one thought anything of it at the time.

Returning to the Palace in the Royal Coach, the Prince blamed the Princess for losing the way. 'Okay, then, *you* do the map-reading!' she snapped back.

It turned out that the two were not made for one another.

The Princess liked *Hello!* and Wham! and anything else with an exclamation mark in its title, though not Princess! Margaret.

The Prince preferred grand opera and the mystic writings of Sir Last Post.

Shortly before the end of their marriage, the Princess of Wails gave a TV interview in which she complained that the Prince was a bad husband and useless at his job.

She thought the broadcast would be a strictly private affair, but millions of ordinary decent Britons tuned in without asking.

She later had a string of boyfriends, among them Captain James Blewitt, international hotelier Norman Bates, millionaire playboy Dodo Flayed and senior surgeon Dr Hannibal Lecter. But none proved suitable.

Andrew and Freebie

The Queen's second son Andrew met his wife Freebie at a bun-throwing party.

'Will you marry me?' he said, throwing a bun at her.

'Oh, yah!' she replied, catching it in her mouth and eating it.

To celebrate their wedding, the Queen gave them the title Duke and Duchess of Yah.

'Hang on, Mummy – how will we *ever* remember which of us is which?' said Andrew.

The two solved the problem by wearing lapel badges whenever they went out. But sadly, at the swimming-pool one day, the Duchess removed her clothes and completely forgot herself.

Since their divorce, the Duchess has learnt to love herself, and the Duke has learnt to love his golf, so they are both very happy.

It's a Royal Lock-Out

Fed up with the rapid multiplication of the Royal Family, the Queen encouraged them all to put on fancy dress and splash each other on television. She believed this would show the public what she had to put up with.

On their arrival back at Windsor Castle, they found themselves locked out. It emerged that ordinary decent Britons had not been impressed by their antics. Inside the castle, the Queen judged *It's a Royal Lock-Out* a brilliant success.

Prince Edward went on to set up his own TV production company, Absent TV. He explained he had no plans to cash in on his name and would be treating a wide variety of subjects unrelated to the Royal Family.

Absent's productions included: *The Beatles and the Royal Family*; *When Humphrey Bogart met the Queen Mother*; *Prince Edward on Princess Margaret*; *Princess Margaret on Prince Edward*; *Prince William and Adolf Hitler and Me.*

CHAPTER 64

Food Scares

Throughout the Eighties, food was a worry. Fifty per cent of ordinary decent Britons were clinically obese and told to eat less. The other 50 per cent were anorexic and told to eat more.

It turned out that even the handful of people who ate the right amount had got it wrong. The MP Egwina Curvy got very eggcited. She warned that, from now on, eggs should be eaten with semolina.

No one liked semolina so sales of eggs slumped, causing farmers no end of eggspense. Some eggsperts felt the scare was eggsaggerated so Mrs Thatcherism thought it eggspedient to make an eggsample of the eggocentric Egwina.

She called her to Number 10 and eggspelled her from the Government for eggspressing such eggstensive, eggstravagant and eggcitable eggsplanations. For a fuller understanding of this period, refer to Eric Hobbskettle's *The Age of Eggstremes*.

In an attempt to calm growing fears of LSE, BMX, ET, CID, PTA, PVC, TTFN and BTM, the Minister for Agriculture, John Seldom Grimmer, had himself photographed tucking into his own daughter.

By the end of the Eighties, most people had taken to eating instant food. The most popular was Not Poodle, best eaten with a spooner.

Shake That Biddy

Inspired by the *Jane Fondle Work-out Video*, ordinary decent Britons took to putting on skin-tight leopards and shaking their bodies up and down to discontent music. Many dancers wore bulbous 'leg-warmers' to make the rest of their bodies look slimmer.

Soon, everyone was on a diet plan. Fashionable diets included:

F-plan Diet: fibre-based, with plenty of roughage such as bran and baked beans.

F-word Diet: foul language-based, with plenty of rough words such as damn and b**** b****s.

G-plan Diet: furniture-based, with plenty of angular sofas for a healthier lifestyle.

H-bomb Diet: mushroom-based, boosting flatulence for those who like to let off steam.

V-chip Diet: V-Chips with everything. Once installed in the body, the V-Chip can be programmed to block any more unacceptable food from entering.

Y-front Diet: pant-based, for all-over body comfort.

President Bush captured the mood of the moment with his famous election quote, 'Read My Hips.' Health-food shops sprang up around the country, including Spud-U-Like, for stomachs, and Cell-U-Lite, for thighs.

CHAPTER 65

Sir Geoffrey Who? Throws a Hissy

After ten years, Mrs Thatcherism's mild-mannered Foreign Secretary, Sir Geoffrey Who?, began to resent the way she could never remember what he had just said. So he stood up in the House of Commons with a view to saying something memorable.

He chose as his subject a game of cricket he once played. He closed the speech three and a half hours later with a long tale that shook the House of Commons into a deep sleep:

It is rather like sending your opening batsmen to the crease and after due consideration of every possible outcome, and with respect for the umpire, who, through dint of both talent and experience has probably earned it, and certainly, I might add, deserves it, and finding, the moment the first balls are bowled by the opposite side, and at this juncture I should point out that whether this occurs before or after one's own side has had a chance to bowl is frankly irrelevant, that, now where was I?

To the sound of thunderous snores from all sides of the House, Sir Geoffrey Who? concluded,

It is now quite some time since I have had the pleasure of donning my own cricketing whites and playing an innings or two of the aforesaid game, but the fact remains that the time has come for others to consider their own response, and that of others, but primarily their own, as others will have to make up their own mind, to the tragic conflict of loyalties with which I myself have wrestled, if that's not putting it too strongly, for perhaps too long, or, on the other hand, perhaps not long enough, I'm hardly the one to judge.

Michael Vaseline was the first to realise it was over, and took the opportunity to throw his cat into the ring. Norman Turbot, a former air hostess, got on his bike and looked for work.

The Last Days of Mrs Thatcherism

After many years of denials, Michael Vaseline finally issued a denial of his previous denials. He announced that he had been unanimously persuaded by himself and his comb that together they would make a much better Prime Minister than Mrs Thatcherism.

Mrs Thatcherism called in her loyal Ministers one by one to ask them what they thought of her. Each told her she was absolutely marvellous, but that she'd possibly even be that little bit more marvellous if she left and never came back.

She took the hint, opting to make a dignified exit from Downing Street howling in tears, hammering on the windows and waving a blue hankie through the back windscreen of her locked car.

But the Conservatories did not choose Michael Vaseline to take her job. Instead, they preferred to pick someone who didn't seem to want it so much. They had had enough of Memorable Prime Ministers for a while.

So an Unmemorable Prime Minister took her place. But no sooner had he entered Downing Street than he found she was still there, hiding behind a curtain, refusing to budge for another seven years.

TEST PAPER VII

The 1980s

1. Where is your Exclusion Zone? Do we all have one?

2. Was the International Monetary Fun? If not, why not?

3. Imagine you are a member of Mrs Thatcherism's Cabinet. It is 21 November 1990. She calls you into her office and asks you what she should do. Do you:

(a) tell her;

(b) change the subject;

(c) cross your fingers and tell her she'll go on until well into the next millennium;

(d) remember an urgent appointment and say your goodbyes?

4. Which of these is *not* an Olympic sport?

(a) Ponting

(b) Denning

(c) Hambling

(d) J. K. Rowling

(e) Hawking.

5. Which of these would you rather do?

(a) Think the Unthinkable

(b) Sink the Unsinkable

(c) Wink the Unwinkable

(d) Clink the Unclinkable

(e) Stink the Unstinkable.

6. Attempt to forget each of the following: Teresa Gorman; Andrew Neil; Cabbage Patch Dolls; TVam; Amadeus; the Rubik's Cube; *Noel's House Party*; Bros.

7. *Either* Explain the Westlife Affair in no more than 3 words, or Lie back and think of Brittan.

8. Source A:

'Frank, we have been friends for over fifty years. Equally importantly, as my legal adviser you have proved to be a shrewd advocate.'

[from *Kane and Abel*, by Jeffrey Archer]

  (i)   Say this line out loud
  (ii) Say it again, only this time try to make it sound natural.
 (iii) Forget it.

9. (i)   How could you make Norman Fowler?
   (ii) Explain Howe.
  (iii) Why was Jim Prior?

10. What is the difference between Saatchi and Saatchi?

11. Which is the odd one out? Black Monday; Tuesday Weld; Black Wednesday; Black Thursday; Man Friday.

12. How soon is now? Give reasons.

THE NINETIES

Age of Dusk, Age of Dawn

The 1990s divide into two equal halves. The first half lasts seven years. The second half lasts three years.

From 1990 to 1997, Britain finds herself led by an Unmemorable Prime Minister; everything goes from bad to worse. But in the second half, from 1997 to the dawn of the New Millennium, Britain turns overnight into a vibrant young, modern country, and leaves all her troubles behind her.

As 1999 turns to 2000, ordinary decent Britons up and down the country set off to work with a spring in their step and hope in their hearts, lustily singing with one voice their brand new National Anthem: 'Things Can Only Get Bitter'.

At last history has come to an end, and we can all rest happy.

1990–97: Dusk

CHAPTER 66

Five Causes of John Minor

In the Years of Despair, Britain was governed by an Unmemorable Prime Minister. Today, he is forgotten for the following unmemorable reasons:

(i) *Not Being Her.*

As time went on, John Minor was widely suspected of not being his predecessor. It was an accusation he may well have denied, but no one can remember.

(ii) *The Citizens' Chatter.*

The Citizens' Chatter gave all citizens the right to phone a Moan Hotline. They would then be guaranteed an automatic recorded apology. If they didn't hear one within ten minutes, they could phone another Moan Hotline to complain about it.

(iii) *Black Wednesday.*

One Wednesday in 1992, the Chancellor of the Exchequer, Noman Lament, found he was in the REM, a technical term meaning Rapid Eye Movement, the dream state. So Lament stripped off, jumped into his bath, and sang 'I Who Have Nothing' at the top of his voice to stop anyone else entering.

(iv) *Egwina Curvy.*

Some years later, it occurred to the Tory MP Egwina Curvy that she might well have had an affair with the Unmemorable former Prime Minister, but she couldn't remember. The Unmemorable former Prime Minister protested that he had already told his wife about the affair, but she had forgotten all about it.

(v) *His Vision*.

The Unmemorable Prime Minister once told his Party Conference of his vision of an England full of warm beer and old maids biking to Holy Communion through the hedgerows in the morning, pissed.

CHAPTER 67

A Memorable Vice Chairman

Margaret Dribble writes:

Jeffrey Archer was not his real name: he was born Winston Spencer Churchill.

He broke the four-minute mile aged fourteen on the very same day that he was awarded a first-class honours degree from Oxford University. This meant that, sadly, he wasn't available to collect his Légion d'Honneur from President de Gaulle for services to the French Resistance. But, as luck would have it, President Kennedy agreed to attend as his official representative.

After a brief spell as drummer with the Beatles, Archer was elected unanimously to Parliament, rising fast through the ranks to become leader of the Conservative Party and then Prime Minister. Not only was he the first teenage Prime Minister, but also the most successful and best-loved.

He left Parliament to concentrate on writing novels, for which he won the Nobel Prize for Literature in 1979 and again in 1980, but he refused to let this interfere with his career as one of England's finest fast bowlers. As Commander of the British Armed Forces, he oversaw the recapture of the Falkland Islands, and, later, the liberation of Iraq.

A small misunderstanding with an attractive young intern called Monica did little to dent the real love and affection he inspired among people of all nations. His emergence from prison in South Africa after twenty-seven years as a political prisoner was greeted with jubilation from all around the world.

'I greet you in the name of peace, democracy and freedom for all,' he said, upon his release. Lord Archer continues to be seen as a living symbol of hope by people of all colours and creeds.

Anus Horribilis

In 1992, the Duchess of Yah was photo-graphed with her financial adviser frolicking naked near a swimming-pool. The Queen later described this as her 'anus horribilis'.

In her Christmas message, she appeared more than usually depressed. She said:

Modern communications make it possible for me to talk to you in your homes and to wish you a Merry Christmas and a happy New Year, for what it's worth. Speaking personally for a moment, I've literally had it up to here. If it's not one thing, it's another. And it never rains, but it pours.

These techniques of the wireless and television may be modern, but the Christmas message is timeless. It's a message that says that, whether you live in a stable or a palace, your family can be a perfect nuisance. I do not intend to name names, but they know who they are, and it is, I believe, high time they bucked up their ideas. The sooner this year is over the better.

Sometimes I don't know why I bother. I wish you a merry Christmas. But not them: why should I?

Two Financial Disasters

Lloads of Llondon
Lload's of Llondon was an age-old institution founded on the economic theory that the only thing the rich lack is more money.

For centuries, you could become a Member of Lloads only if you could prove you had too much money. On joining, you would be guaranteed lots more.

But overnight this all changed. Members were forced to post their money to Lloads, rather than vice versa. It was something they had forgotten to insure against.

Boring Brothers
Boring Brothers was an ancient city institution. Their part of the City had been run on Boring lines for many hundreds of years, and the bank looked as if it would continue to be Boring for many years to come.

The Borings themselves were now so rich that they vowed never to mention the vulgar subject of money. So they hired people off the streets, dressed them in fancy blazers and told them to go out east and gather it in for them. One of these was a sixteen-year-old called Nit Leeson.

Nit went out east in his fancy blazer. Then he began spending the Boring Brothers' money. They imagined Nit was using their money to buy more money for them, but in fact he was using it to buy less money, which wasn't the same thing at all. When they woke up, they found he had got through their whole fortune with only a back-to-front baseball cap to show for it.

It was a financial disaster to beat all others. Once again, Britain led the world.

The Daylight Lottery

John Minor decided to introduce the Daylight Lottery. This encouraged poor people to donate money so that the rich could enjoy their opera in greater comfort.

The Daylight Lottery made poor people poorer. One or two became richer, but television documentaries proved that this only made them unhappy, so no one really minded.

CHAPTER 68

Back to Bostik

In the years of disaster and despair, many little-known Tory MPs were discovered paying prostitutes cash to ask them questions. In a memorable speech, Jonathan Aitken vowed to wield the 'simple sordid truth'. But this turned out to be a tactical mistake.

At the same time, the Tory Party began doing the splits on Europe. In 1995, to ease division, John Minor hit upon the brilliant idea of standing against himself for the Leadership of his Party. He told himself firmly to 'put up or shut up'. He then decided to do both. After a fierce campaign, he won, and immediately conceded defeat.

By the onset of the 1997 General Election, all the remaining Conservative MPs had resigned in disgrace. This left the Prime Minister to ride around the country alone on a soapbox begging people not to tie his hands. Under the slogan 'Back to Bostik' he attempted to glue his party back together again, but without success.

The Conservatives lost; but it was a good ten years before they realised.

Three Memorable Sayings by Thingy

(i) Considerable.
(ii) Quite considerable.

(iii) When the final curtain comes down, it's time to blame
Margaret Thatcherism.

1997–2000: Dawn

CHAPTER 69

An Historic Arrangement

The moment he died, John Smith became the most popular
leader in the history of the Labour Party. It immediately
rallied round him.

But the Party was forced to come to a difficult decision:
many thought he should be replaced by someone still alive.

The two contenders, a young couple called Tony and
Gordon, went out to dinner at an historic restaurant called
Gravitas to decide on who should be the next Prime
Minister. Under a clever deal, each man came away thinking
it was him.

The Third Way

Labour's economists discovered an entirely new way to save Great Britain. It was called the Third Way. Only very clever people knew what it was, or where to find it.

Asked about the Third Way, they explained that:

1. There are two Ways ahead of the Third Way: the Second Way and the First Way, but not necessarily in that order.
2. The Third Way comes after the Second Way, but before the Fourth Way.
3. The Third Way comes before the Fourth Way but after the Second Way.

Following a successful rock concert at the Festival Hall, Tony Blur was voted Prime Minister. 'Ask me my three main priorities for government, and I tell you – Education and Education,' he announced on the doorstep of Number 10.

Six Causes of the 1997 New Labour Victory

(i) The Tories had all resigned in disgrace.
(ii) And Tony Blur played the guitar and wore jeans.
(iii) And there were going to be no more wars.
(iv) And no more scandals.
(v) And everyone would agree about everything.
(vi) And New Labour were going to make everyone incredibly happy.

CHAPTER 70

A New Young Britain

Tony Blur set out to build a new Britain. After coming to power, he made this historic plea to the people of Britain:

> Everywhere you go in this great nation, seek to look modern, to speak modern, to be modern. Away with those old shoes. Away with those brown slacks with the underheel hoops. Away with those dusty old long-players by the Seekers. We want a Britain of New Shoes. New Slacks. New Seekers.
>
> Look, Britain can be unbeatable. Make the good that is in the heart of each of us serve the good of all. May your days be merry and bright. And may all your Christmases be white. Have I told you lately that I love you? Let the sunshine in, the sun shine in. How do you do what you do to me? If I only knew! If I knew what you're doing to me, I'd do it to you. Knock three times on the ceiling if you want me. Twice on the pipe if the answer is no.

Tony Blur's first goal was to make Britain new and young again. For instance, many of the nation's peers had become derelict and had started falling into the sea. So New Labour's mission was to let them be swept away and to replace them with new, disposable peers.

A Caring Prime Minister

In 1997, after the Princess of Wails was killed in France, the new Prime Minister caught the mood of the public by calling her Princess Di. 'She was an Austin Princess,' he sobbed, 'and that is how she will stay in our hearts and in our memories for ever.'

'Anything more to add about her?' asked a journalist.

'About who?' replied the new Prime Minister.

Wave of Inventions

The reign of Tony Blur was famous for its numerous discoveries and inventions. One of these was the theory of the Big Ban, which said that most things should be banned.

Another memorable invention was Bottled Water. From now on, instead of getting their water straight from their taps, ordinary decent Britons could insist on having it bottled in distant factories and transported to shops so that they could go out and buy it for a lot of money.

PlagueStations and GloomBoys were invented to save ordinary decent British children the bother of having to go out and play. Now they could become Olympic champions without ever having to leave their sofa.

For adults and children alike, the Mobile Telephone was a revolutionary invention. It had a Good Side and a Bad Side. The Good Side meant you could cancel appointments with other people at the last minute. The Bad Side meant that other people could cancel appointments with you at the last minute. Txtg mnt chldrn ddnt nd vwls nymr.

Everywhere, there was a rise in Global Warning. Every day, there were new global warnings about killer viruses, killer waves, killer drugs, killer icebergs, killer meat, killer vaccines, killer killers and other possible causes of imminent death. At first, these Global Warnings were frightening, but after a while people began to enjoy them.

A Cultural Renaissance

Tony Blur paved the way for a new young cultural renaissance. This came to be known as Rool Britannia. It consisted of:

The Spice Girls
Until The Spice Girls came along, pop groups had consisted of either:

(a) people who could sing but couldn't dance, or (b) people who could dance but couldn't sing. The Spice Girls set out to change all this. Their members consisted entirely of (c) people who couldn't sing and couldn't dance. It proved a winning formula. The five of them squawked and flapped their arms roughly in time. This gave birth to the term 'Gull Power'.

Oasis

Under New Labour, a new pop group came along, called Oasis. It consisted of the two elderly Gargler brothers, Loin and Mole. Their names became synonymous with Cruel Britannia.

It was easy to tell which was which. Loin was the brother who drank too much and was abusive whereas Mole was the brother who was abusive and drank too much. The two brothers shocked ordinary decent Britons by behaving like rock stars.

They swore, didn't shave, wore old clothes and burped. They were hailed as a breath of fresh air. They were proud to have written all their top ten hits themselves. These included 'Hey Jude', 'Yellow Submarine', 'Hello Goodbye' and also 'The Ballad of John and Yoko', which Loin said was about him and his girlfriend, Pasty Kissit.

BriTart

During the Years of Hope, lots of exiting new Young British Artists (YOBs) revolutionised the art scene. They became famous for being nearly as famous as people slightly more famous than themselves.

Their work was collected and displaced by Screaming Lord Saatchi, a former advertisement, and Sir Rotter, Director of Tat Modern, a former art gallery converted into a warehouse.

Every year, the Turnip Prize was awarded to the YOB who had become famous for stuffing the most people and/or animals in the past twelve months.

The YOBs included:

Damien Hearse – celebrated for ironically employing staff to kill, cut up and frame large animals, then coming up with wordy titles for them all by himself.

The Shipman Brothers – identical doctors from the North, internationally celebrated for ironically doing away with hundreds of old people in a post-modern way.

Traces Semen – known as the BriTart. Gained international acclaim for living in an ironic tent with all her boyfriends and refusing to change the sheets.

New Young Television

Ordinary decent Britons now preferred to relax by watching people who were leading more boring lives than their own. This was known in the trade as Fly on the Wall television, as it was like watching a fly on the wall.

The most popular of these was *Big Bother*, so-called because it was too much bother to switch off.

This was followed by *Celebrity Big Bother*.

Soon, other reality programmes joined it including:

Big Boater – twelve celebrities are shut up in a straw hat
Big Banter – twelve celebrity unknowns aren't allowed to stop talking
Big Baster – twelve overweight celebrities sit around sunbathing
Big Barker – twelve celebrity dogs are shut up in a kennel.

A Cake-up Wall

Ordinary decent Britons were all fat from eating too many chips. The few who were still thin were all given their own TV shows so that everyone else had a chance to get their breath back.

Under the slogan 'Things Can Only Get Batter', John Prescott, Lewd Neighbour's speeding lunarist, developed a punning clan for a major cake-up wall to butt cack on beamy crumbs and dizzy frinks, and leave all the batty fits to sun wide.

From now on, no one would ever be overweight again.

Under New Labour, an international team called Poshunbex won the World Shopping Championship. After extensive training under tropical conditions, Poshunbex proved capable of running down Bond Street and stripping all the shops bare in under four minutes.

Poshunbex then gave birth to three little shoppers. They christened them John Lewis, Harvey Nichols and Boots.

CHAPTER 71

Faith at the End of the Twentieth Century

In the Years of Hope, the decline in faith was halted for ever. On Sundays, people would flock from far and wide to the Swedish Church of Ikea. Once there, they would repent of their sins by walking round and round in circles in silence, touching as many different objects as they could.

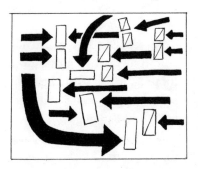

Finally, they were forced to stand in line for hours and hours bearing great weights. Their penance continued at home, where they were made to weep in front of twenty-six different-shaped

fig 1: Floor plan of IKEA Croydon, and troop advances at the Battle of Omdurman.

pieces of wood, an instruction map with no words but 103 arrows, and not quite enough nuts and screws.

The Envy of the World

To celebrate the year 2000, a giant Dome was to be built at Greenwich. It would be the envy of the world.

The Minister Peter Meddlesom boasted that the Millennium Gnome would be capable of holding:

- 18,000 double-decker buses
- 131 Albert Halls
- 3.8 billion pints of beer
- 12,000 Nelson's Columns
- 800,000 mopeds
- 11.2 million deck-chairs
- 90 million anoraks (medium size)
- 17.5 billion cup-cakes
- 2 million doctors (laid end to end and stacked)

In a major speech, Meddlesom revealed he had already extracted firm promises from corporate sponsors of three mopeds, a gallon of beer, seven deck-chairs and a dozen packets of cup-cakes, and that discussions for a double-decker bus were ongoing.

With less than a fortnight to go, the Government decided to divide the Dome up into five 'zones', carefully distributing the various bits and bobs around each zone, including,

Learning Zone: let the potentiality of the imagination be released in this hugely educational empty space

Mind Zone: explore the endless uncluttered horizons of the human mind in this intellectually stimulating empty space.

Faith Zone: a chance to sit and meditate on the nature of spirituality in this serene empty space.

Play Zone: discover the nature of play, where anyone can be anything, in this endlessly exiting empty space

O Zone: strip off a few more layers and relax in the new-found warmth.

History Ends Yet Again

At the dawn of the New Millennium, Britain was wonderfully new and young and modern and vibrant once more.

Henceforth, nation would live in peace with nation, and all the people would be living life as one.

There would be no more war and no more strife. Disputes would be settled with a nod and a wink and a cheery thumbs-up.

From now on, Tony Blur and his friends in New Labour would build the world a home, and furnish it with love, grow apple trees and honey bees, and snow-white turtle doves.

Ordinary decent Britons would work together in perfect harmony, all standing hand in hand, and you could hear them echo through the hills for peace throughout the land.

At the stroke of midnight, all the most brilliant and attractive Britons joined arms in the splendid New Millennium

Dome, happy in the knowledge that this magnificent creation would act as a shining beacon to the whole World.

It was the End of History, and the dawning of a new error. From now on, nothing could possibly go wrogn.

Up to the End of History

1   Source A:
    And even in the gas and electricity he talks about Government and Treasury particularly have always imposed a kind of energy tax on them, forced them to charge more through the external financial limits the negative role he talks about which is a tax on those industries

John Prescott, speech to the House of Commons,

7 May 1998

Read Source A, then ask the following questions:

   (a)   Come again?

   (b)   I'm sorry?

   (c)   Could you repeat that?

2. 'Things can only get b--ter'
    What are the missing letters? If you have not answered in 45 minutes, this paper will self-destruct.

   (i)   es

   (ii) it

(iii) un

(iv) ut

3. Is Dessert Storm better served in a dish or a cocktail glass?

4. Translate into English, giving meanings: Swampy; Bez; Gazza; Bono; Eminem; Suggs.

5. Source B:

'I have slowly come to realise, and somewhat unwillingly, that I will have a crack at the leadership as soon as I can. Partly because I am in touch with real people, partly because I can offer some leadership and view of the future. I look at rivals like David Mellor and like me better.'

from *Diaries 1987–92*, Egwina Curvy.

Read Source B carefully before answering the following question:

Which of these two statements is the more accurate:

(i) 'Egwina Curvy was Prime Minister from 1988–1997. Her premiership will be remembered for its leadership, clear view of the future, and ability to remain in touch with real people.'

(ii) 'Egwina Curvy resigned from her job as Junior Health Minister in December 1988. She recently became one of the first people to be voted out of the television programme *Hell's Kitchen*.'

6. Which Conservative leader described himself as 'The Quit Man' before resigning?

7. Why did dringe binking become a clause for concern or whatever?

8. Giving examples where necessary, describe how you would go about being
   (a) tough on rhyme, tough on the causes of rhyme
   (b) tough on grime, tough on the causes of grime
   (c) tough on mime, tough on the causes of mime.

9. Why did Ellen Highwater go to sea in a cut-off-meringue?

10. Why was Clare Short? What did Robin Cook? Why did David Blunkett? Which was Jack's Straw? What made Gordon Brown?

11. Spot the obvious mistake: Sir Mark Thatcher.

12. Why does it always rain on me? Discuss.

Before finishing this book, read it all the way through one more time. Cross it out. Your mind is now furnished with a complete understanding of all the modern history that never quite happened, and some that almost did.

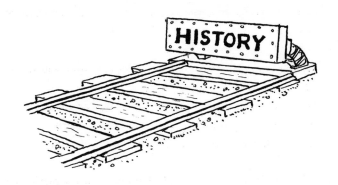

THE BEGINNING

THANKS

It was Nick Davies's idea. Robert Harris and Francis Wheen both encouraged me to give it a go. Caroline Dawnay sewed up the deal. Kate Cayley lent me hundreds of GCSE exam papers. Ian Hislop and Hugh Massingberd read the book through and made lots of good suggestions. My thanks to all of them, and to Henry Jeffreys and Nick Welch, too.

It has been a real treat to have a book illustrated by Ken Pyne. Barely would I have finished each chapter before scores of drawings, all beautiful, would be winging their way to my desk.

It is no joke living with a humorist, but my wife Frances continues to do her level best.

Finally, my thanks to W. C. Sellar and R. J. Yeatman, whose classic *1066 and All That* remains as fresh as a daisy after seventy-five years. This book is an attempt to recapture something of its undying spirit of nonsense and fun.

C.B., Aldeburgh, April 2005